D1306395

As I
Remember It

As I
Remember It

A Memoir of Persistence,
Tenacity and Humor

Theresa Wanta

ISBN: 9798772032527

Cover photo: Elsa Frettem
Photo p. 117: Tom Ordens

Set in Adobe Garamond Pro and printed in USA

For Lorayne and Richard Radde

and their daughter Rachel

Table of Contents

Preface

The 1950's were a conservative time. Most people were conformists, followed the rules and worried about what others might think of them. It must be remembered that where and when I grew up the value system was different from today and different from large cities. Children were to behave, money was to be saved, adults to be respected and most of all, we were taught to be responsible. Character was paramount; personality frosting on the cake. Grandchildren were just grandchildren, loved but not an obsession. Where I grew up children were loved in a practical fashion, that is, fed and clothed, but not shown a great deal of affection.

At the age of seven I was considered capable of doing field work eight hours a day with an hour off at noon. School was my salvation because there the teachers praised my work, I had access to books, and I was exposed to children of different ethnic and religious backgrounds, though all Caucasian.

As I Remember It is just that, written as I remember those years, not as my siblings or parents may have remembered them. I will leave it to them to write their own memoirs.

Everything in this memoir is true, although everything that is true is not in it, nor should it be. Each child experiences their parents differently based on gender, birth order and fluctuating family circumstances. Each child's temperament and personality elicit different responses from parents.

Since there is a price to pay for every choice one makes, one may as well march to their own drummer. As Katherine Hepburn said, "If you please yourself, at least one person is satisfied."

Every author faces the problem of selection. I have chosen incidents that I thought would be entertaining, informative or relate to a historical context and have searched my memorabilia to be as accurate as possible. Often I refer to books I've read because I've always felt my early years were out of society's mainstream and books helped me see how I fit into the "big picture."

Finally, it must be said that there is always the temptation to see the past in today's context, through the lens of the present moment, our own subculture and experience. In fact, I wonder if it is possible to do otherwise. I try to present life and thought as they were in the context of that particular location and period of time.

1

Convent Years

At the young age of fourteen, I made up my mind to become a nun, and in 1956, I entered the convent. As a public school student, I had been impressed with the nuns who taught us Bible School for two weeks after school let out each spring. They seemed so lively and happy.

In my altruism and idealism, I wanted to do something extraordinary with my life and to serve a broader spectrum than an immediate family. I found the aesthetics of spiritual life appealing and wanted to serve God in the best way possible. Did I like boys? Of course, I did, otherwise where would be the sacrifice? Besides, the convent did not want to be a refuge for those who were disappointed in love. In the 1950s, before the Vatican II Council had been convoked, the Catholic Church promoted voluntary self-denial as the highest vocation for a woman, and I strove for the best.

On a less altruistic note, I wanted to get away from farm work, was enticed by the higher social status of nuns, and could think of no other way to get a college education. One of the occupations listed in the convent recruitment brochure was "artist," and that was what I genuinely wanted to be. Finally, I considered the religious life to be the only way to be assured of a place in heaven.

I joined the Sisters of St. Joseph of the Third Order of St. Francis in Stevens Point, Wisconsin, located 30 miles from my home. It was one of three provinces with a general motherhouse in South Bend,

Indiana. The hallmarks of the Franciscan rule were poverty, humility, and simplicity. Unlike a contemplative order, it was an active order whose original mission was to teach Polish immigrant children. In 1901, it had seceded from an order serving German immigrant children in Milwaukee. At one time one had to be of Polish extraction to enter this order.

One of the entry criteria was willingness to work. When my mother came to that question on the application she said she wasn't sure what to say. For the question on motivation, I wrote I wanted to serve God, do good, to save my soul and the souls of others. Other requirements included a $50 dowry and a well-defined list of clothing and toiletries. Nothing fancy or silky in the clothing department, though on the list was a black umbrella, considered a luxury at home. I received it in May for my fourteenth birthday. Like a blessing, it rained that day, so I ran around the house to try it out.

ON A SUNDAY LATE IN August, my parents drove me to the convent. Constructed in 1903, it was a sturdy building with walls 18 inches thick, surrounded by tall virgin stands of white pine.

Everything was spotless. The woodwork held a faint scent of

The convent building as it appeared when I entered in 1956. At the time it also housed an academy for girls.

furniture polish. I left my parents in the visiting parlor and climbed the four flights of stairs to the dormitory with its appropriate dormers, to change into the aspirant's uniform. The term "aspirant" referred to the first stage in the process through which an aspiring young woman became a religious. An older aspirant accompanied me while I dressed

in a small "cell" with its wooden chair, bed, and washstand. The cell was enclosed by white cotton curtains suspended from narrow gauge pipes connected to each other crosswise in a grid, which in turn were attached to the ceiling by vertical pipes at the intersections of the grid.

As an aspirant, August 1956-1959.

Through the curtain I asked my new companion whether to put on the white tee shirt first or the corset waist. Tee shirt. The corset waist was nothing more than a muslin vest with a multitude of snaps down the front, supposedly a substitute for a bra. Then came a blue cotton half-slip that went down to just above the hem of the uniform. The uniform was a box pleated, long sleeved, black wool serge dress that hung six inches below my black stocking-clad knees. A short cape came down to my elbows, topped with a Peter Pan style white plastic collar with a tiny grosgrain bow at the snap closure. A wool beret, worn primarily in chapel, completed the uniform.

I went down to model for my parents, gave them my secular clothes, and posed for snapshots taken by my mother with her Brownie camera. The trunk with the required personal belongings was unloaded and I said goodbye. My family did not show emotion and did not hug. By the fact that my mother took pictures was in itself an indication that it was an important event. I was looking forward to this new adventure. I wanted to please God. I wanted my parents to be proud of me.

All of the aspirants arrived at roughly the same time, and each of us was assigned a space the width of a uniform in a large common closet where we hung our Sunday, daily, and work uniforms. Under this we placed our Sunday shoes on a shelf that went around the wall of the closet, and beneath which we put our suitcase. Our trunks went down to the basement.

Each newcomer was assigned a "Big Sister" who answered any questions we might have. Sometimes on a feast day during our first year, the "Big Sis" gave us a token gift such as a religious medal or holy card depicting a religious image.

The nun in charge was called "Mistress." While the term has more dubious social connotations in secular life, in religious life it was merely a title of authority over those in training. There were 23 in our group, the largest in the history of the congregation. Those in training progressed from aspirant to postulant to novice. We were, however, referred to as "little ones." This felt odd since I was accustomed to farm responsibilities, was now in high school, and was 5'8½" tall.

Except for the provincial homes, every convent house was associated with a parish, school, or hospital and was referred to as a mission. Each had a sister superior who answered to her respective provincial mother superior. The three provincial convents of Chicago, Cleveland, and Stevens Point were subject to one General Mother who held the highest authority in the order at the motherhouse in Indiana. These top administrators had council members with whom to consult on matters of legislation. Because we were a papal rather than a diocesan order, the General Mother answered to the pope, the ultimate CEO.

My new life had begun. At 5:00 every morning, we rose to the sound of a bell, and at 10 p.m. we retired. As we rose, an appointed postulant announced "Jesus lives", to which we responded, "My God and My All." This was to motivate us right at the start of our day to live for Christ. By 5:20 we were groomed, dressed, and in chapel for meditation. We could get ready quickly because we never had to decide what to wear. All the cell curtains were pulled back, neatly pleated. We learned to make a bed with square corners, the way they

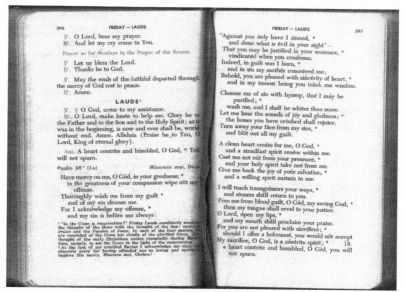

A Short Breviary **that contained the psalter.**

do in the army. The bedspread had to be pulled so taut that a coin could bounce off it, if we had had one.

A half hour of meditation was followed by the recitation of the psalms and Mass. Prime, Terce, Sext, None, Matins, and Lauds were sets of psalms chanted in Latin in the morning, followed by Vespers and Compline in the evening. This pattern of recitations, known in the Middle Ages as "The Hours," is called the breviary, the official prayer book of the Church. We used the shortened version, referred to as the Little Office, because we didn't have time to pray all day. Although technically these were to be chanted at one, three, six and nine in the morning, we prayed them all together at a reasonable hour because we were an active teaching order. Now I see some similarity to the prayers that devout Muslims chant throughout the day.

I soon realized that the Psalms, with their parallel imagery, were among the most beautiful poetry forms: Psalm 90: "With his pinions he will cover you/ and under his wings you shall take refuge"; Psalm 29: "You changed my mourning into dancing/ you took off my sackcloth and clothed me with gladness" and Psalm 114: "The cords of death encompassed me/ the snares of the nether world seized upon me." In addition to the Psalms, we recited community prayers in the morning and evening, often composed by less poetic Western minds.

We cleaned our assigned area between mass and breakfast. After a breakfast eaten in silence, we attended the all-girls' Catholic high school across the street, which was operated by our own order. It was supported by the contributions of the diocese, local parishioners, student tuition, and the free labor of our teaching nuns. We were not allowed to talk to the secular girls except in class discussions. We were a group apart and were not to socialize with them. Many years later I learned that these girls perceived us as aloof because no one had informed them of the rules we followed.

We were not allowed to talk to the professed teaching nuns outside of class either. An exception was made on holy days and feast days such as that of our patron, St. Francis. Most of the nuns fled the onslaught of aspirants on those occasions, though there were always a few who deigned to indulge our hunger to talk to adults. I never understood that article of the constitution. Why would we, who were aspiring to become nuns, be segregated from those who might offer guidance and inspiration?

We followed a program that allowed us to finish high school in three years instead of four; we were under pressure to get out and teach since at that time there was a shortage of nuns in Catholic schools. We had six classes a day, substituting extra courses for study periods and taking summer crash courses during June and July. I wore out the seat of my underpants sitting in those wooden desks so much. Much to my dismay, chemistry was omitted as were art and drama. But there were piano lessons.

General silence was observed throughout the day except when it was necessary to speak, as when we taught or attended classes or during recreation. When we met other aspirants, postulants, or nuns in the corridors, we greeted them with "Praised be Jesus Christ" to which they responded "Forever, Amen." This was omitted during Grand Silence, which was kept from after evening prayers until after breakfast. Evening prayers always ended with the beautiful

"Magnificat," the canticle of the Virgin Mary, sung in Gregorian chant with outstretched arms.

To break Grand Silence was considered a serious matter. Sometimes, as we studied in the conference room, we wrote notes to one another and got the giggles. Then up to the dorm at 9:30 and lights out at 10 p.m. The appointed older postulant went around sprinkling each of us with holy water. We could always identify the Mistress by the sound of the beads worn at her side when she came to the dorm to check on us. She would glance a flashlight into each cell, not detecting that sometimes an aspirant lay fully clothed under the covers. After a novice became professed and received rosary beads, she sometimes startled herself by the sound of her own beads.

A total of 32 postulants and aspirants slept in one dorm, separated from one another by the white curtained cells. There were two bathrooms for the entire dorm. Each night we filled our enameled pans and plastic tumblers with water and took a sponge bath in our cell. We used water from the tumbler to brush our teeth and spat into the pan. After emptying the pan, the containers were filled with fresh water and placed on our washstand for morning use. There's nothing as ascetic as washing your face in cold water on a winter morning. In the adjacent dorm where the novices slept, a crust of ice formed in their pans. Steam heat clanging through the pipes and radiators culminated in a mighty, lengthy hiss, a precursor to the bell that signaled it was time to rise.

Occasionally, those of bolder temperament sneaked down four floors to the kitchen to bring up cookies for the rest of us, though I have to say, it was pretty difficult to knock on the cell curtain to distribute them. The more daring among us played tricks on the others. Once, after a safe length of time had passed after bed check, someone began throwing smuggled corn flakes over the tops of the cells. There was a lot of giggling. Remember, we were in our early teens. One aspirant went to the general closet and got her umbrella to put up over her head as she lay in bed.

Other pranks included short-sheeting a bed and placing a hand broom under the covers at the foot of a bed which felt like an animal to the touch of a bare foot. Hiding someone's underwear or the entire contents of a washstand would result in tardiness at morning prayers for the victim, who would have to ask for a penance without giving away the prankster or prank. I never played these tricks for fear of being sent home.

Eating between meals was not allowed except for snacks at 4 p.m. on school days, and at 10 a.m. and 4 p.m. on weekends. We never ate outside the dining room except for special occasions when we had a treat in the conference room. This was acceptable, since it was all made clear before we entered the convent.

Meals were eaten in silence while we listened to spiritual reading, or more accurately, reading books about spiritual topics. Each of us took turns for a week at a time to read the assigned book. Sometimes we were required to take turns reciting the Rule of St. Francis by memory during the meal. This was supposed to keep us inspired during our day. The home cooked meals tasted good; much of the produce was grown on the premises. But it did seem strange to have Spam or cottage cheese for breakfast. The meals were served family style, and afterward, one pan with soapy water and one with clear rinse water were brought to the table to wash the dishes. We competed with one another to see which table would finish first. Each person's silverware was then wrapped in a cloth napkin with the dinner plate turned over it. The glass was inverted in the cereal bowl, as was the cup on the saucer. Thus, the table was set for the next meal.

All aspirants, postulants, and novices sang in the choir for daily Mass, which the entire community attended. We rendered polyphonic melodies as well as Gregorian chant, either with accompaniment or a capella. Although seldom performed today, I still appreciate these Gregorian melodies, also known as plain chant. Many of them are contained in a sizeable book called the *Liber Usualis*. For major feast days we sang special liturgical arrangements such as Palestrina's *"Missa Solemnis"* or "Mass of Junipero Serra," both of which are polyphonic pieces, as opposed to a plain chant composition such as "Missa Angelorum," which was used for everyday Mass. Afterward at breakfast, we performed a special selection such as *Arcadelt's "Ave Maria"* for the entire community.

On these feast days we were allowed to converse during meals. To break the silence at the beginning of the meal, the superior or mistress announced, "Praised be Jesus Christ!" to which we responded "Forever, Amen, God bless you, Sister, good appetite to all!" This was recited in Polish before I entered the order. The meals were especially good on those days, and sometimes community prayers were shortened. In the evening, we performed a choral reading, a play or talent show to entertain the rest of the community, mostly the administration and older and infirm nuns.

When a Sister died,

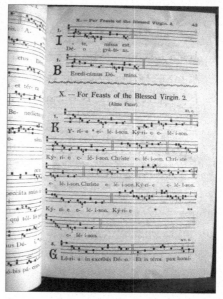

A page of Gregorian Chant from *The Liber Usualis.*

another nun bathed and dressed the deceased member so no mortician touched her except for embalming. A wake was held in the convent parlor where friends, parishioners, and relatives paid their respects. We missed classes to sing for her funeral. It was always the Gregorian Requiem that was chanted at Mass followed by "In Paradisium," also a Gregorian melody. I loved that piece. At the cemetery, "Serdeczna Matko," (Beloved Mother) a traditional Polish Marian hymn, was sung in three-quarter time. It was sure to bring on the tears if they weren't flowing already. I once served as a pallbearer, and doubt I will have that privilege again. I remember thinking how wonderful to be able to do this last thing for Sister Adelicia, a nun whom we dearly loved, admired, and respected.

We were allowed to write to our families once a month. It had been made clear that our incoming and outgoing mail would be censored. Sometimes the Mistress wrote a small complimentary note to our parents at the end of the letter, such as "She's a gem." We were not allowed to maintain correspondence with former friends except at Christmas. During Advent and Lent we were not allowed to write letters even to our families, but made up for it by sending an especially long one at Christmas. Any letters we received were reserved until the upcoming holiday. Phone calls were never allowed, either to or from our families. That didn't matter to me because my family didn't have a phone anyway.

On Good Friday we knelt while we ate breakfast, which on that day was only bread and coffee. We felt very holy, you can be sure. On Easter Sunday, we had the most varied and delicious homemade Easter breads I have ever eaten. There was even chocolate bread! Once we had poppy seed cake. Not having tasted it before, I thought the poppy seeds were coffee grounds but ate it anyway, thinking it was meant to be a form of penance. The kitchen Sisters baked wonderful "babka" for breakfast at Easter. This was a raised loaf of bread made of sweet dough with dried fruit inside. Dozens of "babkas" were delivered to our benefactors as tokens of appreciation.

If we transgressed the constitution or customs deliberately or accidentally, we accused ourselves individually before the mistress, asked for a penance, and then kissed the floor. Usually the penance was to say some "Our Father's" or "Hail Mary's." The professed Sisters did the same, and the one who taught biology said that to avoid germs she kissed the floor through her scapular—a cloth worn over the habit that falls to the hemline in front and back. After we became novices or professed nuns, sometimes the collar or crucifix was confiscated for a more severe infraction. Although humiliating for the transgressor, this evoked silent compassion from the rest of us. I never did find out what merited this kind of mortification.

The prime regulatory policies were in the Holy Rule, the rule of the Third Order of St. Francis Regular, which we never broke since it included the vows and would be cause for dismissal. We followed the articles of the Constitution, 318 of them, as closely as

CHAPTER I – SPIRITUAL EXERCISES

THE ORDER OF THE DAY

1. RISING, 5 A.M. The Sisters should rise punctually at the first sound of the bell and begin the day with the following ejaculation: LONG LIVE JESUS! (Niech Zyje Jezus). The others answer "My God and My All." ("Bóg Mój i Moje Wszystko.")(300 days indulgence)

2. If any Sister is obliged to remain in bed longer because of weakness or sickness, the Sister next to her in the Chapel should inform the Superior of the absence. If the Superior herself cannot be present at the morning prayers, or at other Community exercises, the Vicar should start the prayers and take care of the other duties of the Superior.

3. The Crucifix, habit, cord and veil are blessed; therefore, in putting these on or taking them off, the Sisters should kiss them reverently. (For the kissing of the habit in gratitude for the grace of a religious vocation, there is an indulgence of 5 years. Pope Leo X.)

4. The Sisters should always be clean and modestly attired; affectation in dress is a breach of the religious spirit and against holy poverty.

5. Before they go for morning prayers, the Sisters should uncover their beds and open the windows to ventilate the cell or dormitory. In dormitories and cells, everything should be in perfect order.

6. MORNING PRAYERS, 5:20 A.M. The Sisters recite their morning prayers in common in the chapel, or some other oratory designated for that purpose.

7. Immediately after the short morning prayers follows the MEDITATION, lasting a half hour. (Plenary indulgence once a month for those who make a half-hour meditation daily, or at least a quarter of an hour.)
At the end of the meditation, the leader says an OUR FATHER, and the ejaculation, All for Thee, Most Sacred Heart of Jesus. (300 days indulgence each time).

8. THE LITTLE OFFICE OF THE B.V.M. – The Sisters will recite the Little Office in common; if there are fewer than four Sisters, it is recited privately. (Indulgence 7 years. Plenary indulgence once a week).

9. The following order is observed in going to receive Holy Communion: The Professed Sisters, the Novices, the Postulants, according to the instruction given in our Constitutions. To the Visiting Sisters, the Mother General or Provincial or Local Superior assigns places.

10. Thanksgiving after Holy Communion should last at least 15 minutes.

A page from the custom book.

possible. Some of them were merely housekeeping rules. The most minor rules which were listed in the Custom Book also numbered in the hundreds, and were often broken because they were so detailed and inclusive. Sins belonged in the confessional, but it was hard to commit any in a convent environment. One couldn't even confess to having an argument since we kept silence so much. The priest

-31-

CHAPTER XI - RECREATION
A. GENERAL REGULATIONS

178. The time assigned for recreation should serve to produce physical relaxation, renewal of spiritual strength, and intensification of the bonds of Sister love. Recreation should be sanctified by good intention and remembrance of the presence of God.

179. All the Sisters should spend recreation time in the evening in common, as much as possible, in the recreation room. They may converse happily, enjoying innocent jokes, or playing some games. Playing cards is not suitable enjoyment for religious. The Sisters must avoid playing cards with seculars or with priests, because it leads to transgressions and violations of convent regulations.

During recreation the radio or TV may be put on some good programs; the radio may be used also when important educational or religious programs are presented, or when the Holy Father or the President speak on some occasion. Each time, however, the Sisters must have the permission of the Superior.

Outside of recreation, the Sisters should not have the radio or TV on without the permission of the Superior.

Television sets will be permitted in the Community room of the convents. However, the Sisters may not purchase their own sets. If a set is donated, it may be used under the direct control of the Superior, for religious, educational, and cultural programs.

The superiors may not permit the Sisters to view programs during the time prescribed for community prayers. We are religious and not secular teachers. When we deprive ourselves of enjoyment for the sake of Jesus, He will reward us a hundredfold. Let His Cross serve as a book from which we can derive all necessary knowledge.

The Sisters are not allowed to attend movies or concerts at the local theaters, unless they go with children or this entertainment is planned for the Sisters only, or is approved or sanctioned by the bishop of the diocese.

180. It would be a transgression against the Constitutions and sisterly love if some Sisters were to isolate themselves, and were to spend their recreation exclusively with one Sister.

181. During recreation the Sisters should:
1. Cease all mental work such as studying, painting, or correcting of papers.
2. Refrain from boisterous laughing and shouting.
3. Avoid sitting with crossed legs.
4. Avoid making sarcastic and caustic remarks, asking inquisitive questions and playing unpleasant tricks on others.
5. Avoid praising themselves because of their family, talents, wealth, influence of their relatives.
6. Refrain from criticizing Superiors and their commands. It is best not to say anything about others unless we can mention something ... and praiseworthy about them.

Regulations from the constitution.

confessor said listening to nuns' confessions was like being stoned to death with popcorn. We lived a lifestyle based on rules that were centuries old, while in the 1950s the rest of the world was rapidly changing. By the 1970s, religious life was changing drastically. As John Fialka states in *"Sisters, Catholic Nuns and the Making of America"*, *"*Rigid rules of bureaucracy began to dull the spirit in convents, taking away the creative opportunities of the frontier days and making sisters' work a mere habit in a habit, not a license to do good works."

We spent every Sunday morning in silence, reading, praying, and walking the beautiful grounds. We were not allowed to do homework until after lunch. The purpose of silence was to cultivate internal communication with God, i.e., to "live in the presence of God" and to avoid earthly distractions. It also served the practical purposes of saving time and avoiding arguments—not a minor thing considering there were so many women living under the same roof.

On the first Sunday of every month we observed Grand Silence all day—a one day retreat. In the morning we accused ourselves of our faults, based on the Custom Book, before our entire group. This was done while we all knelt beside our desks in the conference room, facing the front. The purpose of this exercise was to develop humility. Sometimes we burst into giggles because the faults were so absurd and comical in the telling.

We accused ourselves of accidentally slamming a door, breaking silence, and looking out the window through curiosity. One of the aspirants who worked in the kitchen could barely get it out that the tomatoes she had been carrying slipped out of her hands and fell down the dumbwaiter. This young woman thought everything was funny and did not seem to feel guilty about any infraction. Once she got into a tug of war with the Mistress, each pulling the door in opposite directions. She was eventually asked to leave the order; we later learned that she had gotten married and given birth to twins, which we hoped had every bit the same sense of humor.

Because we were in training, no social activities were allowed outside the convent grounds. This was all right with me because rural life had been relatively isolated except for church, school, and visiting nearby relatives. I liked being with so many girls my age and of varied backgrounds, and besides, there were flush toilets. There were countless books available, although certain books such as *Gone with the Wind* and *Doctor Zhivago* were off limits. The spiritual and intellectual aspects of this life were attractive to me. Our affections and desires were sublimated and directed toward Christ, or in secular terms, we were in love with God. I liked the silence and did not find it difficult to observe. Today my friends find that hard to believe. I did not feel lonesome for my family and felt far less restricted than most of the girls did. This was an exciting adventure. I had always known there was a bigger world and this was it.

For summer recreation we walked the grounds. I liked to listen to the wind sighing in the tall pine trees. In winter, their boughs caught the snow and enthralled my soul. Toward the back of the convent grounds, there was a grotto of Our Lady of Lourdes with porous rock imported from Italy, a playground, a tennis/volleyball court, an arbor, and a cemetery. Recreation after supper was at a designated time and usually consisted of a mandatory group activity such as walking, listening to music, ice skating, or playing volleyball.

Not having had indoor plumbing at home, I was curious to see what was in the tank above the toilet. Once, during outdoor recreation, I feigned having to use the restroom. No one was around when I lifted the lid with its hairline crack off the tank. To my dismay, it broke in two and fell to the floor! I examined the internal mechanism, carefully replaced the lid (now lids) and told not a soul. The next day I noted the pieces had been taped together. My guilt was assuaged two years later when the entire building was renovated, including the toilets.

Sometimes we had a party to celebrate some religious feast. While I liked the social aspect of these planned activities, I was disappointed that reading was not allowed during recreation. No one was allowed to go off in two's or develop "particular friendships" so as not to distract from our primary relationship with Christ. Recreation was followed by spiritual reading, then evening prayers. I was assigned the duties of porter, which entailed checking all the doors and windows in the cavernous basement after prayers every night—alone. I was always a bit uneasy but only once found an unlocked window.

During recreation in winter, we darned our black cotton stockings while listening to classical music. Some who hated darning used black marker pens on their skin so the holes wouldn't show. For the first time I was being exposed to classical music. It was the most beautiful music I had ever heard, and my love of it persists to this day.

On winter weekends and days off from school we scrubbed, waxed, and buffed hallways, dining rooms and the chapel on our hands and knees, except for the hallways, which we scrubbed and buffed with a hand-held machine. If one was not experienced with this machine it would take off on its own! There were also kitchen and laundry duties. We spent Saturdays peeling vegetables for 150 nuns plus those in training at the provincial motherhouse. Since we were not allowed to talk, we took turns reciting the decades of the rosary. When I saw relatives during summer vacation, they asked, "What do you do all day?" I suppose if one were raising a family it was difficult to imagine how nuns spent their time.

On weekends in early summer, we mowed the lawns, raked leaves, and trimmed hedges. We cleaned the older nuns' rooms, cleaned out the attic, and worked in the garden. While some complained of the work, those of us who came from farms thought it was a breeze. One of my tasks was to trim the grass around the tombstones and shear the cedar hedges surrounding the cemetery. I liked doing that, reading the names of the deceased nuns on each tombstone as I trimmed, thinking how this was a service I could perform for those who had gone before us. On each tombstone was engraved, "Sister Mary _____ asks for a Hail Mary." On the older tombstones it was engraved in Polish. During the earlier years of the 1900s there were many nuns who died young because of the tuberculosis epidemic. In fact, our provincial home had a separate quarantine location for a TB sanitarium about three miles away where, incidentally, the noted poet Jessica Powers resided during her illness.

In fall, an after-school and weekend chore was to wash windows inside and out in the four-story convent building. As we sat on the window sill washing the windows on the outside, someone always held on to our legs from the inside to make sure we were safe. The music room had two gigantic, beautifully symmetric Boston ferns flanking the hand carved wooden figure of St. Michael the Archangel. During my first year, having just finished the outside of the window, I leaped in from the windowsill, my long legs kicking over one of those ferns. Surprisingly, I was not reprimanded. Years afterward, a small fern stood across from the large fern: an asymmetrical testament to my lack of grace.

On Tuesdays the novices rose at 5 a.m. to work in the laundry. They received communion before Mass, omitting the Mass itself, ate a hurried breakfast and were on their way. The aspirants and postulants helped with laundry after Mass and breakfast but before classes. We also helped during noon hour. There were sheets and sheets and sheets (at least 150 x 2) to be hung outdoors in fair weather and down in the convent basement on rainy days. When they had reached just the right degree of dampness, the sheets were gathered and pressed through the mangle as were other flat items such as handkerchiefs. The mangle consisted of many huge hot cylinders covered with padding and cotton cloth. I remember the brand name "Troy" in gold letters outlined in black on the dark green side panel of the machine because it reminded me of the Trojan horse. The entire laundry was operated by steam heat and there was a tall, round chimney outside to prove it. After school, those with more experience fed the mangle while the rest of us, six abreast, received the pieces on the other end. The pressed laundry was hot to the touch and resulted in much blowing upon and shaking of fingers.

Sister Julia, a tall kindly nun in her eighties with laughing brown eyes and her head tilted to one side ran that laundry for as long as I can remember. "All for the glory of God," she often said. I liked her best of all the nuns because she was truly spiritual yet so human and practical. To me this was the epitome of sanctity. Inspired by her, I decided that I would always be human and approachable when I became a nun. I believe I achieved this because after Vatican II, when the nuns dressed in secular clothes, people could not believe I was a nun. The quotation of St. Ignatius appealed to me: "The glory of God is a man (read "person") fully alive."

A bakery stood behind the laundry building. Their freestanding positions greatly reduced the possibility of fire spreading to the main convent building. Long wide rows of compost stretched off behind, where we disposed of organic matter daily and then covered it with leaves. Each row had an indentation down the middle to catch the rain, and every spring the oldest rows were distributed in the garden. Next to the compost was an incinerator for burnables. The Sisters referred to it as "the Kaiser," not surprisingly, given the history of Poland.

The convent was a self-sustained operation. In the provincial home there were nuns who were housekeepers for the chaplain, sacristans, shoemakers, seamstresses, bakers, cooks, gardeners, printers, bookbinders, and enviably, one artist. As an order, we operated and administered our own hospitals and schools. There was little we didn't do for ourselves outside of carpentry, plumbing, and electrical work. After I left the order, I could not believe that some of these functions were solely the domain of men.

During those first two and a half years of aspirancy we went home for the month of August. I usually spent that month painting the tall, white, clapboard farmhouse, outbuildings, and machinery. My siblings were afraid to climb the ladder to the tip of the old part of the house. I was just as afraid as they were, maybe more so, but I was also afraid to admit it. And once they had excused themselves from the task, it fell to me. I also helped out with the usual chores which included weeding the huge garden that kept the family fed throughout the winter. This wasn't so bad because I knew I would be gone again before the dreaded potato picking season began.

If we wanted to return in fall, we had to petition in writing to do so. The order did not want anyone there against her will. This was not such a far-fetched concern, considering that in the early days of the order, parents would offer a daughter partly, as they believed, to assure their own place in heaven, and partly to have one fewer mouth to feed.

For the rest of the year we were allowed four visiting Sundays with our families. Though I respected my parents, and knew they led busy lives, I couldn't help feeling disappointed on those occasions when they didn't come—our farm was only thirty miles away—and I envied girls whose parents traveled almost 200 miles from Milwaukee to see their daughters. Friends were not encouraged to visit or write lest they become sources of temptation to "return to the world." We were reminded that while we were in the world, we were not *of* the world. Today I am still fairly detached from material things.

On Saturdays, we had a sign-up schedule for baths, which took up almost the entire day since there were only two tubs and each person had a half hour in which to bathe and clean the tub for the next person. It was also the custom in all bathrooms throughout the building to wipe out the sink after washing one's hands, out of respect for the next person who would use it. The rest of the day was taken up with aforementioned cleaning, yard work, choir rehearsal, and confession.

It seemed that there was never enough time to study, and no time to read for pleasure. No books were allowed in our "cells" at night. We were not allowed to frequent the dormitory during the day, but it didn't matter because there was little time or reason to go up there. We were required to account for any activity outside the community room except for classes. In retrospect, I believe this may have been because we were minors and the community felt responsible for our whereabouts and well-being. We were not allowed to listen to the radio, watch T.V. or read newspapers since these were perceived as distractions to our spirituality while we were in the formative stages of religious life.

The Sunday and daily uniforms, and later the habits we wore, were made of wool serge, while the work uniform/habit was of black cotton. To save the cost of dry cleaning, every year before Easter we took apart the daily uniform, (and later on, the habit) seam from seam, washed and ironed each piece, and sewed it together again. This was done only once a year because the extensive underwear and washable dress shields acted as barriers to soiling the habit itself. Spot cleaning was done in the interim.

Later, when we wore black veils, we washed them whenever we wanted, and while they were barely damp, folded them between two smooth and very heavy pieces of tag board and slipped them between the bedspring and mattress. After a week, Presto! We had perfectly pressed and creased veils. There were two precautions to be taken: a veil too damp became moldy; the use of corrugated cardboard resulted in a corrugated design impression on the veil.

We had five sets of underwear, but only three sets were allowed to be put in the laundry each week. The rest was hand laundered in a bucket and hung in the attic during our "spare" time. If any item was too soiled, it was returned to us to be hand laundered before being put into the laundry. This baffled me since I didn't see any point in sending clean clothes to the laundry.

In the practice of poverty, we carried not even a dime with us. In that same spirit we kept no gifts. This included money, food, or any other item. Rehearsing for the vow of poverty, we submitted the gifts we did receive for general use while we were still aspirants. Gifts of food were shared with all and only with the permission of the Mistress. At Christmas we were advised to suggest practical gifts from our families. Out of kindness, the Mistress allowed us to request one item to keep for ourselves. In the spirit of community the rest was shared with those who needed it. This was not too difficult since by now we were accustomed to self-denial and had learned to sublimate our desires.

Whenever we went out in public, we went by two's. As we walked, we recited the rosary and practiced "custody of the eyes." This meant we kept our eyes downcast. We were not to talk to seculars except when necessity or charity demanded it. We were not allowed to frequent the public library. We did not attend movies at the theater but viewed preselected rented films in the assembly room on a feast day. On our name days, which replaced celebrating birthdays, we sang "Happy Name Day" to the tune of the "Merry Widow Waltz." Often we composed religious lyrics set to melodies of popular songs.

After two and a half years as aspirants, we became a postulant for six months. The etymology of the word is Latin, meaning "to demand." This meant we were more serious about our decision to become a member of the order. All rules were stricter for postulants, who studied the Rule and Constitution more carefully. The black beret was replaced by a short black veil with a white plastic half-crown piece at the front. Following that stage, we became novices for a two year training period during which we lived the vows of poverty, chastity, and obedience, though we did not yet officially profess them.

The concept was not just to give up money, marital love, and one's own will, but to free ourselves and direct our energies to better love others and serve their needs. Love of God didn't count unless translated into service of others. Many, if not most people, did not understand the practice of these three vows, so myths evolved. Our lives and our works were generally not viewed as an act of love. It seems that too much altruism breeds suspicion. Priests were admired for practicing celibacy while nuns were ridiculed for remaining virgins. Movies and images of nuns depicted us as naive nitwits or ruler-wielding child beaters. As John Patrick Shanley, director of the play and later the film, *Doubt*, stated, "Many orders of Catholic nuns have devoted their lives to serving others in hospitals, schools, and retirement homes. Though they have been much maligned and ridiculed, who among us has been so generous?"

As a postulant from February to August, 1959.

The novice wore the complete garb of the professed nun except that her veil was white instead of black and she didn't wear rosary beads. The headgear consisted of a six-inch-wide plastic band that covered the forehead to just above the eyebrows and wrapped around to the back of the head. The top of the band was attached to a semicircular piece of very heavy tag board over which the veil was pinned with heavy, five inch straight pins with beaded ends to protrude beyond the plastic band, resulting in a square shape. It took some practice to get these in at the correct angle. If you knocked the veil against the wall while cleaning house or getting into a car, you were literally "bent out of shape." This headgear was attached with small straight pins to either side of the starched cloth wimple which was pinned tightly on top and in back so that only the face was exposed.

The black, wool serge habit extended to within three inches of the floor, and had long, wide sleeves with four-inch-wide cuffs. Sleevelets worn under the long sleeves were merely a cuff attached to a sleeve held up at the elbow by elastic. These were removed when we did heavy cleaning or with permission when the weather was very hot, or to obtain a suntan up to our elbows.

A white woolen cincture was worn about the waist with three knots in it to signify the three vows. A scapular, a straight piece of cloth which hung from the width of the shoulders and extended to the length of the habit in front and back, was worn on top of the habit. A large round plastic collar circled the neck and closed in back under the veil. A crucifix was suspended around the neck and showed just below the collar. If we anticipated being hugged on visiting Sunday, we were cautioned to remove the collar to avoid cracking it.

Novice from August 1959 to August 1961. Feeling a little awkward wearing the habit for the first time.

A big celebration was held for the investiture of novices. Family was invited and a reception meal prepared. Aspirants and postulants rehearsed special hymns months in advance. The ceremony conducted by the bishop was quite dramatic. Each prospective novice wore a white wedding gown and veil with the habit folded in her arms. We were given a new name chosen from among three we had submitted. This was a new practice since in the past, the novices were given names without personal input. That may have accounted for some of the rather strange names such as Sister Mary Adelgunde, Appolonia, Crispiana, Dionysia, Egidia, Eulodia and Praxidia given in the past. Sometimes we made fun of these names and invented

31

'Brides of Christ.' I'm in the back row, third from right. We were the largest class in the history of the order.

comparable names such as "Sister Kunegunda" or "Valigoudahey."

The name change signified leaving the old self behind and taking on a new spiritual identity. Surnames were not used as a further guarantee of anonymity. We did not learn which name was to be ours until the bishop announced, "So and so, you shall henceforth be

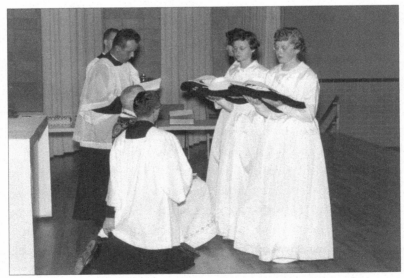

Receiving the habit and a new name. I'm second from the right.

called Sister Mary—." But our names were distributed on little strips of folded paper, and as we processed into the chapel, I guessed my new one while holding the tiny sliver of paper between the fingers of my folded hands. The imprint of the typewriter keys showed through in mirror image and spelled "Sister Mary Joyce." It was my second choice, the first being "Christa."

Once our new names had been announced we left the altar and changed into our habits. Since we had no idea how to wear the headgear, a professed nun of our choice helped us dress. When all were ready, we processed back into the chapel.

Then began two years of novitiate training, the first of which was held at the motherhouse in South Bend, Indiana. Novices from all three provinces were trained at this location. We took the Soo Line, traveling through Chicago at midnight, and since we carried no money on our person, were each given a dime for the pay toilet in the depot. I couldn't imagine having to pay to use a toilet.

This year of novitiate was a time of testing—the "boot camp" of religious life. Not only did we study the meaning of the three vows of Poverty, Chastity and Obedience, we were trained in matters of form: how to walk like a nun, talk like a nun, and eat like a nun. We learned to walk with smaller steps with our hands clasped at the waist, (no swinging of arms or swaying of hips), and to speak in modulated tones. And we learned to slit the sides of a banana with a fork, peel back the top like a sardine can, and eat the banana as we sliced it from its cradle.

I found this year stressful since my every action was scrutinized. All of us were assigned impossible amounts of work, most of it manual. This was to test our mettle. We hoisted up and pinned back our long skirts, pulled back and pinned our veils. To test our obedience, tasks were done and undone according to the will of the Mistress. We dug up myrtle from one end of the grounds and transplanted it to the other, only to learn later that the group preceding us had done vice versa. We swept the brick driveway eleven abreast, which reminded me of what I had learned in fifth grade about the Dutch, who not only swept, but scrubbed their cobblestone walks.

I was lucky to be chosen as the artist representing my province, and I worked with an artistic and highly intelligent general council member by the name of Sister Mary Theobold. She patiently taught me to use the air brush—a pen-like instrument to which a small reservoir of colored India ink was attached. When the compressor was turned on, air was forced through the reservoir, producing a fine colored spray that I manipulated to decorate greeting cards. These were designed for the administration for feast days and name days.

One of my drawings for a feast day card.

We never left the premises except for doctor or dentist appointments. An exception was made when we went to an orchard outside the city to pick the largest, most delicious peaches I have ever tasted. There was only one visiting day during the entire year for which my mother came by Greyhound bus.

We asked permission for each bar of soap and tube of toothpaste, presenting the sliver of soap and empty tube as proof that we were in need. The purpose of this was to practice poverty and instill humility. We faulted ourselves for every act short of perfection. We never knew when we would be called in under the pretense of having done something wrong, even if we had done nothing wrong. We now studied the constitution more assiduously. We were again schooled to live in the presence of God and to sublimate our work and our thoughts. We strove for perfection as future "Spouses of Christ" and came up with the ditty: "If the plural of mouse is mice, then the plural of spouse must be spice; that makes us the Spice of Christ."

If a novice left the order during this time, we were not told of it until after she had gone, so we never got to say good-bye. The mistress came into the conference room with the veil and headgear of the departed novice draped over her hand and waved it in front of us. "This is what happens if you don't pray enough," she would warn us, or "this novice picked her nails during prayer," or "this novice was too strong willed." If few novices left, the mistress was told by the mother general that she wasn't being tough enough on us.

The second year of novitiate was spent back at the provincial home among familiar faces. It was a solid year spent in college study. The usual tasks of laundry, cleaning, and care of the premises offered a change of pace from our studies. I thoroughly enjoyed that year. The chaplain, our avant-garde theology instructor, introduced us to the theological works of Gerald Vann, who established criteria for a just war; Karl Rahner, who advocated returning to the sources of Christian faith, i.e., scripture and writings of Church Fathers; and Karl Barth, known for Word of God theology. All of them, along with Edward Schillebeeckx, influenced Vatican II.

I liked Reinhold Niebuhr's tenet that the Church is the Church only when it exists for others. Just "me and God" isn't enough. Dietrich Bonheoffer, an anti-Nazi dissident who died in a concentration camp, mused about the emergence of a "religionless Christianity." I liked that concept. And Hans Küng questioned the infallibility of the pope.

This chaplain placed various Church doctrines in their historical context, analyzed their contemporary spiritual significance, and spoke of the blossoming of a morality based on love rather than fear. I found his views attractive, but they were the opposite of what I had learned in childhood. I should not have been surprised when he was requested to leave by the provincial administration because of his "radical" ideas. Yet his was the best theological training I had ever received and it served me well throughout my career teaching religion to school children.

Due to such studies, we were well prepared for the onset of the Vatican II Council. When we began to teach, we unfortunately posed a threat to older parish priests who were not interested in updating their own knowledge or interpreting the Vatican II documents to their parishioners. For example, they would state: "From now on, we

A study in anonymity: the first religious profession of the members of all three provinces at the motherhouse,1961. I barely recognize myself in the last row, 5th from the right. The bishop's head appears to overlap my collar.

will stand when receiving Holy Communion." They did not feel the need to explain the rationale for that change: to emphasize that our faith was based on the resurrection, not the death of Christ, and that standing was the resurrection position.

I made my first religious profession in 1961 along with the other novices, formally taking the three vows for one year, with the intention of renewing them one year at a time for five years:

"I, Sister Mary Joyce, vow and promise to God Almighty, the Blessed Mary ever Virgin, to Saint Joseph, to our Holy Father, St. Francis, and to all the Saints, and to you, Reverend Mother, to observe the Rule of the Third Order of St. Francis approved by our Lord Pope Pius XI, and to live in Obedience, Chastity, and Poverty for one year according to the Constitutions of the Congregation of the Sisters of St. Joseph of the Third Order of St. Francis."

We were now temporarily professed Sisters. We exchanged our white veils for black ones and began to wear the beads of the Franciscan Crown suspended from the cincture at the waist. The Franciscan Crown, an adaptation of the usual Catholic rosary, was a chain of seven rather than five decades of beads. (The origin of praying the beads dated from a time when peasants were illiterate. Instead of reading the Psalms they substituted a "Hail Mary" for each Psalm. Since there are 150 psalms, the complete rosary is the recitation of the set of 50 beads three times.)

We wore a crown of silk white flowers on our heads that day to signify the joy of becoming the spouse of Christ, who in a larger sense represented the Mystical Body of the Church. The ceremony was held at the motherhouse in Indiana where we had spent the first year of our novitiate.

The family of each sister attended, including those from farms, with the exception of mine. In the absence of my family, I was invited by another sister to join hers. Then it was back to the provincial home for the second year of college, which I found as enjoyable as the first. After completing that year, I received my first assignment.

I began teaching with no practice teaching under my belt (or cincture, as the case may be). I taught forty-five students, three grades at a time, at St. Mary's Parish in Stanley, Wisconsin. We were to find our own rides to our new mission, and not knowing any parishioners, I relied on my parents to drive me there.

I didn't really want to be a teacher—I had hoped to become an artist nun—but at this point the idea of serving God and others superseded personal preferences. As David Rockefeller, in his autobiography, *Memoirs* states, "But as I have learned, duty is liberating. It forces you to transcend your own limitations and makes you do things that may not come naturally, but must be done because they are right." And transcend my limitations I did. Though it's said that one cannot truly switch from one type to the other, I apparently morphed from a quiet, timid introvert to a communicative, entertaining extrovert. Being a nun was really a way of life rather than a job. That is to say, we dedicated our lives to God and the service of his people, which necessarily translated into work.

I felt lucky to have had at least two years of college while some of the older novices went out to teach with only one. We did not own a car because of the vow of poverty and relied on parishioners to transport us for grocery shopping and errands. That makes one wonder who was really keeping the vow. In larger parishes there was a parish car for the nuns' use and a designated driver.

At 20 years of age I was not old enough to vote and was embarrassed that the parishioner who drove the other three nuns to the polls would notice I had not come along. I pulled my wimple forward to try to make myself look older. I feared the parishioners might learn that I was not degreed and did my best to prove their children were being educated by a professional.

As a fully professed Sister in 1961.

It was a small convent. In fact, it had previously been a private residence. The three nuns I lived with were a teacher, who was 40; the cook, who was 71; and the sister superior and teaching principal, who was 60. The superior was not kind to me. I now think it was because I was a beginner teacher, which added to her burden. The irony was that I was originally to be sent to St. Mary of the Angels in Green Bay where there were many young nuns and much enthusiasm, but while waiting for my ride, the provincial mother spied me and re-assigned me.

On Sunday mornings we were not allowed to do any classroom work; we kept silence, read books on spirituality, and prayed. I was under greater restriction than the others because I was still in temporary vows and was not allowed to leave the convent house except for school and church work. Neither was I permitted to visit nuns of my own order in the neighboring town, even accompanied by the fully professed nuns from our house. When the pastor took the nuns on an outing to his cottage, I was not permitted to join them. Left alone one Sunday afternoon, I entertained myself by reading the only secular book I could find: *Webster's Dictionary*.

I was assigned a combined classroom of third, fourth, and fifth

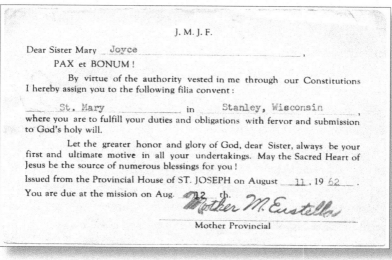

J. M. J. F.

Dear Sister Mary _Joyce_ ,

PAX et BONUM !

By virtue of the authority vested in me through our Constitutions I hereby assign you to the following filia convent :

St. Mary in _Stanley, Wisconsin_ ,

where you are to fulfill your duties and obligations with fervor and submission to God's holy will.

Let the greater honor and glory of God, dear Sister, always be your first and ultimate motive in all your undertakings. May the Sacred Heart of Jesus be the source of numerous blessings for you !

Issued from the Provincial House of ST. JOSEPH on August __11__ , 19 _62_ .

You are due at the mission on Aug. _12_ th.

Mother M. Eustella

Mother Provincial

Due at my first mission assignment, August 12, 1962.

graders—a total of forty-five students. I had never taught a day in my life, and here I had to teach three grades at a time. I had no training except for the admonition that no corporal punishment was to be administered. Not having undergone practice teaching, I had no idea which textbooks to use or what level of knowledge a third, fourth, or fifth grader might have. I asked the forty-year-old nun to help me. She pointed out which books to use for each grade and then told me not to ask her any more questions, because the last time she had helped young nuns, they had turned against her.

During the first day of school I quickly learned how much more material I needed to prepare for the next day. The students didn't know things I expected them to know, and knew things I hadn't expected. I had no idea how to write a lesson plan but was a good organizer. Class preparation was in itself overwhelming as I prepared for fifteen classes every night.

I graded most of the forty-five students' papers myself because the students performed better when they knew I looked at their papers individually. Some classes, such as geography and history, were combined and taught every other year. I felt responsible for the education of these children and was determined not to shortchange them just because I was a first-year teacher. During parent-teacher conferences, I was afraid of the parents until I perceived they were intimidated by me, with my black garb and wimple.

I was so lonely I cried at night. The teaching experience was new and I never knew whether or not I was doing a good job. The two other nuns were impatient with me, sometimes scolding me in front of my class. I was not familiar with parochial school procedures because I had been a public school student. The superior had the TV on continually in the community room where we prepared for the next day's classes. I couldn't concentrate with Mitch Miller and Leslie Uggams performing but was not allowed to prepare in my bedroom because I was still in temporary vows and was obligated to be with the rest of the community. I worried about my performance report and so did not complain. Since I could not confide my misery to the Sisters with whom I lived, I tried to tell the confessor how frustrated I was and how I could not keep up with the work. He said it was God's will. I remembered that is what the priest had told my mother when she had confided in him.

When I didn't have time to adequately prepare for a content class, I assigned a paragraph to be read silently by the students while I read three paragraphs ahead so I could present additional information, thus saving face. We had no breaks during the teaching day except for a quick lunch. We supervised the children on the playground for both recesses as well as the noon hour. Along with this there were the usual daily prayers, meditation, and spiritual reading, which were, in truth, oases in an overwhelming day; a built-in antidote to stress. After I left the order, I continued the habit of meditation and reading to prepare myself for a stressful workday. It seemed that if I could have that bit of time to myself, I could deal with anything.

As an assistant sacristan to the forty-year-old nun, I spent the first part of every Saturday morning cleaning the sacristy and sanctuary, arranging flowers, candles, vestments, etc. This head sacristan scolded me for not knowing how to do things I had not done before. She scolded me for not watering the flowers, and then scolded me when I had, because by then they were past the need for water. Also on

Saturday mornings I taught CCD (Confraternity of Christian Doctrine) to public school students, as I had been taught when I attended public school.

In the afternoon I ironed the priest's linen albs, cleaned my portion of the house, performed school secretarial work, wrote minutes to teachers' meetings that were never held, prepared lesson plans, checked papers and went to weekly confession. I composed and typed review tests for various subjects for each grade and printed multiple copies in purple print on the mimeograph machine. Ironically, I took a correspondence course in practice teaching, which only added to my workload with its useless requirements of writing anecdotal records and such. I had neither the time nor the materials for doing my own art. I despaired of ever drawing or painting again.

We cleaned our own classrooms daily, and since I deplored using teaching time to clean, I worked out a system. At five minutes before dismissal, I got out the wide mop, ran it down the aisle nearest the windows and then asked the children in the first row to move their desks onto the cleaned aisle. I repeated the method for all six rows and then said, "Okay, everybody move your desk back where it was." The students seemed to enjoy this cooperative effort.

When it was our turn to clean up the playground, I asked each student to bring me three pieces of litter. The personal, specific nature of the request gave the chore a positive twist. Some of the younger children became perturbed if they could only find two pieces! During Easter and Christmas vacations we scrubbed and waxed our own classroom floors to save money for the parish. I had to enlist volunteers from the classroom to help on a Saturday. I hated to see children do work that in my opinion was the responsibility of adults. At those times special church services required more time than usual in the sacristy and sanctuary, eating into our class preparation time.

At that time the Church had obligatory fasting during Lent from Ash Wednesday to Good Friday. This meant Catholics were permitted to eat one full meal as well as two smaller meals that together were not equal to a full meal. I knew I could not do this since I was already exhausted. I requested and received a dispensation from the priest.

I prepared for Easter Saturday services all day. Exhausted and depressed, I cleaned up after those services until after midnight. No one asked how I was, how things went for me. I think it was then that I first began to doubt that I belonged there. I sublimated the hardship each day. It wasn't supposed to be easy, was, it? It was supposed to be a sacrifice. I screwed up my courage and persevered.

On Christmas Eve the cook Sister served spoiled liver sausage. I had never had liverwurst before and had no idea how it was supposed to taste. Although I noticed the others had not eaten it, I wanted to appear cooperative, since it already seemed an affront to be young. I was violently sick all Christmas Day. On another occasion, the cook dropped a glass bowl of Jell-O and then served it in small dishes. My tongue ran over the smooth gelatin punctuated by glass shards.

The following year President Kennedy was assassinated. We barely ate as we sorrowfully watched TV the whole weekend. After two years, I asked for a transfer. This was a new development. In the past, out of obedience, we had to stay where we were sent unless instructed otherwise by the Provincial Mother.

For the next three years I taught first grade at St. Stanislaus parish in Stevens Point, now called Holy Spirit Parish. There were many younger nuns at this mission, including a young but experienced nun who taught the other first grade class. Through her kind mentoring I gained confidence in my teaching skills. Besides, I had only thirty-five students and only one grade.

The best part about teaching first graders was their eagerness to learn; they were genuinely upset if a school day was canceled for some reason. They loved penmanship class because I walked around the classroom several times observing each child's paper and offering suggestions. Every child loves special attention. After they learned to read, every Friday afternoon for the last few minutes, I asked a child to choose a book to read before the class. They loved this and were proud they could do it. The Dr. Seuss books were a popular choice.

Although teaching first grade content quickly became boring, I enjoyed this mission because there were many young, intelligent, capable nuns with a good sense of humor. We discussed classroom strategies, theological issues, and, since these perpetually professed Sisters were allowed to read the newspapers, world events. During recreation we argued about social justice issues. I learned that the purpose of discussion is not to prove one is right, but to search together for the truth; I learned that it is essential to define terms, and that opinions are not facts.

We exchanged hilarious stories about our students: "If God is everywhere, is he in the cavity in my tooth?" "Is God in the bathroom?" to which another student replied, "I know he is because my father pounds on the door and says, 'My God, are you still in there?'" We often sang in the parish choir for weddings; the parishioners liked to request "The Nuns' Choir." In every parish, one of the nuns was assigned as the organist, whether she had played the instrument before or not. I can't imagine how stressful that must have been.

The superior related to us as definitely inferior. After she returned from a national educational conference, we begged her to share the ideas presented, but instead she described the soap in the hotel room. Although we had adult responsibilities in the classroom we were treated like children in the convent house. We received lollipops for Christmas. One of the Sisters told me that the superior thought I was a good teacher, but that I shouldn't be told this, because I might become proud. I was grateful for this bit of information; after four years of teaching it gave me my first inkling that I was doing it effectively.

Times were changing, and the two youngest nuns were not as fearful or respectful of authority as I was. When it was time for "The Way of the Cross" Lenten devotions on Saturdays, these two hid in the convent basement. The superior searched high and low for them. As she went to the basement to look for them they sneaked back up and ran ahead to church, kneeling in the pews like angels. After the service she scolded the two renegades. They were not one bit contrite but smiled through the entire reprimand! This further infuriated the superior who confided to us older members that she just didn't know what to do with them because nothing intimidated them.

Again I was sacristan, this time for three clergy. I got up at 4:30

a.m. on Sundays to put out the chalices, vestments, etc. for the 5:30 Mass. After the last Mass at 11 a.m., I ran in to clean up, put away, and rearrange. On weekdays, the nuns attended the earliest Mass and then a later Mass with the students. After teaching all day, I taught confirmation classes on Thursday evenings. At confirmation the bishop congratulated the pastor on how well *he* had prepared the youths. On Saturday mornings, I again taught CCD religion classes to public school children. Since this was probably as hard for them as it was for me, I did my best to make the classes interesting and relevant to their lives.

In 1966, at the age of 24, in the fifth year of my temporary profession, I pronounced my final or perpetual vows. During the ceremony we each received a crown of thorns to wear for the day to signify sacrificing our lives for others and a 14 karat gold ring to represent our marriage to the Church as Brides of Christ. While I kept the silk crown of flowers from my first profession, I threw away the crown of thorns the very next day. The pastor of this parish was invited to participate in the ceremony, held at the chapel in the provincial home. He stood directly in front of me as I pronounced the vows before the bishop. Although I had worked in his parish for three years, the pastor neither showed recognition nor offered congratulations afterward at the reception.

After we became perpetually professed Sisters, we were allowed to visit our parents for a week every five years, and if we had a blood sister in the community, we could go on one another's vacations, making it a vacation every two and a half years. If we had no blood relative in the order we were not allowed to go home alone but had to take another nun with us. We were instructed not to uncover our heads in the presence of family members. During the few times we went anywhere else, we always went in pairs.

In the summers we went to remote rural areas to teach two weeks of Bible school, just as I had been taught when I had attended public school. I was assigned to Armstrong Creek along with the most brilliant nun in our group. During that assignment I bought groceries for the first time. I ordered two pounds of bologna cold cuts for the two of us without realizing how much that would be. (Enough to last us almost two weeks, it turned out). Our task was to prepare the younger children to make their first confession and communion and the older children to study for their confirmation. Whenever I prepared children for confession I emphasized its positive aspects and also how rare the circumstances of committing a mortal sin were. I didn't want them to experience the fear and guilt I had felt at that young age.

These preparations also included meeting with parents, ordering supplies for the ceremonies such as rosaries, prayer books, communion veils, etc., and rehearsing hymns and processions. The children were very well behaved, and the pastors and parents in these outlying parishes were kind and grateful to us. The pastor at the Armstrong Creek mission gave up the rectory for us and stayed with a parishioner during the two weeks we were there. He left his Mynah bird for us to care for. This provided a never-ending source of amusement as we could never predict when the bird would pierce the silence with a wolf whistle.

After the two weeks of teaching, we attended summer school at St. Norbert College to work on our bachelor's degree. We always took the maximum number of credits allowed for the summer, usually nine. The rules of silence were relaxed; we listened to popular secular songs on the car radio such as "Green, Green" by the Christy Minstrels and "Morning Has Broken" by Cat Stevens. Summer school gave us the opportunity to exchange all the gossip of who had left the order, which parishes were kindest to the nuns, and which superiors were the toughest.

Following summer school, we went on retreat for a week during which time we uttered not a word except in prayer or hymn. In some years the retreat master, usually a Franciscan brother, was inspiring; in others insipid. One of them addressed us as "Dear Little Sisters." In any case, we were stuck with the designated preacher for a week. One brilliant young nun was so bored during his lectures that she surreptitiously read an entire book on theology. She got in trouble for that.

At the end of the week we received our fall assignments. We never knew whether or not we would return to our previous "mission," as the parish was referred to. In order to be prepared, we packed our trunks at the end of every school year. If we received a transfer, it would be shipped to our new mission; if not, we would unpack it again for the following year. If we were transferred, we never got to say goodbye to the previous parishioners. This fostered the spirit of detachment not only from secular relationships, but from advantages offered by different parishes and clergy, which varied by location. Some parishes and priests were kinder to us than others, and it was easier to make friends with some parishioners. Examples: the clergy in Green Bay bought roller skates for all the nuns (24), obtained Green Bay Packer tickets for them, and in some parishes, they bought tickets to shows or concerts for them as a gesture of appreciation. The idea was not to get attached to these parishes.

In 1967 I was transferred to Blessed Sacrament Parish in Milwaukee where Father Groppi had led Black protest movements a few years earlier. I taught five classes of science and spelling on the first four days of the week, and five classes of art and music on the fifth. These subjects were assigned to me because no one else wanted to teach them and I was the "newbie." This was fine with me because I liked science as well as the challenge of teaching music. There were forty-five students in each of three classes of seventh graders and two classes of eighth graders. The classes were arranged homogeneously according to ability. To make for effective classroom control, I memorized 225 names as early in September as I could. Unsurprisingly, the first and easiest to remember were those of the brightest and the naughtiest.

For science classes I persuaded the Parent and Teacher Association to purchase a lab table and supplies. After all, I reasoned, if they could afford to buy football uniforms for the seventh and eighth graders, surely they could put some funds toward science equipment. They did. The lab table used for demonstrating experiments and a magnifying microscope which could project live images in color were wonderful. A student volunteered his pet goldfish (carefully wrapped in a wet tissue) so we could observe the red blood corpuscles pulsing through the veins of its tail. We observed the palisade layer of a leaf and the underside with its stomata, all in living color.

I obtained a beef heart and kidney from the butcher to dissect, and I made use of it to explain the circulatory and excretory systems. If I really wanted to impress the children, after explaining the human systems I would point out that they all worked simultaneously within our bodies without our having to give them a thought. There was palpable silence as the wonder of it sank in. Whenever there was something really complicated like ohms, amps, and volts to explain, I checked out a film from the downtown library. The students loved seeing a "movie." I had to learn to run the Bell and Howell movie projector to do this, and I was proud of the accomplishment.

Because I had little previous knowledge in the field, I prepared for the music classes conscientiously. As a result, the students assumed I had a master's degree in music. I assigned research questions to challenge the best and the brightest, but they were clever enough, in this age before Google, to call the reference desk of the city library and make short work of the assignments. After they finished their entrance exams to college prep high schools, they returned to tell me they were the best prepared musically of the applicants. In those days, even in Milwaukee, the kids could mosey on into the building after school hours or on Saturday to see if their teacher was in. Many of them loved to talk on an informal basis. One student asked, "How come you're so nice after school?" to which I replied, "How come you're well behaved after school?"

I challenged myself to get the students to love any subject they hated. I couldn't imagine anyone not liking school because I had liked it so much. In the end, they even liked spelling class. But at first the brightest eighth grade class didn't bother to study much, because even with one misspelled word on the weekly final test, they would still qualify for an "A." I presented the dilemma to the superintendent who suggested I give them all "B's" since the text was geared toward average students, and they weren't even getting a hundred percent correct on average material.

I wasn't prepared for the fallout. Parents and students alike were in an uproar. After I explained my rationale, every student in that class got every word correct for the rest of the year. To make it more interesting, I had them design crossword puzzles from the weekly vocabulary list, thus reinforcing definitions. Having them exchange these with one another also freed me from checking their work. They were quick to pick up on technical errors in the construction of the puzzles and resolved them faster than I could have.

The Sister who taught seventh and eighth grade math and history boasted of how responsible her homeroom class was; how they were all in order, said their prayers, and recited the "Pledge of Allegiance" even if she wasn't present. One morning, I happened to pass by her classroom and noted her students were having a high old time until the lookout near the doorway signaled her approach. There was a hush, and with perfect timing the entire class stood up and recited in unison, ".... with liberty and justice for all." I don't think she ever caught on, and I was not about to burst her bubble.

To complete my bachelor's degree in education, I attended classes at Marquette University and Alverno College after teaching and on weekends for what seemed like an eternity. The credits were transferable to St. Norbert College, my alma mater. The students' parents assumed I was working toward a master's degree and I did not disabuse them of that notion. Once, as I prayed with the class at the end of the day, I wore a thin film of a raincoat since I had to dash off to class right after school. After prayers were finished, one of the seventh grade boys remarked, "Sister, it looks like you just came back from the dry cleaner's!"

On a cold Monday morning in late winter, one of the students remarked, "We don't want to be here, and we know you don't want to be here, so why don't we all go home?" Another time, when I was being firm about some point of order, a saucy student remarked, "Oh, come on, Sister, you were young once, too." I was 25.

These students were challenging and amusing. I learned they were fundamentally on my side when the supervisor of schools came to observe my teaching. I was dismayed when she scheduled to be present for my poorest class of seventh graders. To my amazement, these students were unusually attentive that day and participated wildly in class discussions. I was delighted and gratified. After the supervisor left, I complimented them. Their mischievous grins extended from ear to ear.

Myths tend to evolve from mysteries. Always having our heads covered gave rise to the myth that perhaps we did not have hair. One day I stuck a feather between my wimple and cheek to really make them wonder.

By this time, I rarely scolded the class, nor did I send students to the principal's office. I believed that to send students to the office only served to undermine my own authority and indicate I couldn't handle the problem on my own. I had developed methods of control without raising my voice. Usually this meant being well prepared and getting right down to business. If a student misbehaved, I stared at him until he settled down. The boys said, "Do anything; scold me, punish me, but don't stare at me." Another effective technique was to stand near the desk of the offending student. If the whole class wasn't settling down, I noted the time on the chalkboard, and then made it obvious that I was staring at the clock. Soon they began to quiet down. I noted the time again and subtracted it from either their noon hour or recess. After once or twice, they got the idea. I learned none of this from John Dewey in my education courses.

Once, however, in early spring, five seventh grade boys were late coming in from noon hour. Where were the missing boys? It turned out they had been off the school property "whipping matches" in a huge culvert at the end of a sewer. This could have been very dangerous if sewer gases had accumulated in the culvert. Because of the seriousness of the offense, I called the parents to meet at the convent with their sons in tow. Each boy had to report what he had done. That was enough punishment for the boys, and unwittingly for the parents, who were more concerned about who the other parents were than about the offense.

After a year, the teacher's reputation preceded her, so the following year was a breeze. The students all knew who would let them get away with things and who wouldn't. I saved the most interesting projects and activities for February and March, when everyone was getting tired of both school and winter. There was one thing I was adamant about and my students knew it: there was to be no bullying on any level. My mantra was: "How would you feel if someone did that to you?"

To get these junior high students to do what I wanted, I used reverse psychology. When it was raining outside during recess, they inevitably insisted it wasn't raining hard enough to warrant their staying indoors. The next time I wanted them to stay in during bad weather, I insisted they go out. When they protested, I feigned relenting. Conversely, when they didn't want to go out on a dreary but dry day, I just told them they *couldn't* go out, which predictably resulted in their demanding the opposite.

There were so many young nuns at this large parish that they could not all fit in the main convent. The overflow lived in a small house a block away. During my second year there, I was one of the lucky ones who got to live there. We liked it because it was homier with its French windows and cozy rooms. Also there was a bit more freedom, though none of us would think of breaking a rule. We still prayed and dined at the main convent. To take a shortcut, we ran through the paved alley between the rectory and church.

One dark October morning at 5:30 a.m. it was raining as I ran through the alley with my arms full of school books. I forgot about the chain the monsignor had stretched across the alley to deter bikers. I tripped and split my chin. My lesson plans were covered with blood. I missed a half day of teaching, which was to be the only time I missed in ten years in the profession. I called a parishioner to take me to the doctor because I was afraid to ask our designated driver, the scowling cook Sister. When I returned to the classroom that afternoon, the most rowdy students looked up in awe at the four stitches in my chin. It made me mortal.

Afterward, I paid the monsignor a visit to inform him the chain across the alley was a health hazard. He corrected me and said it was not an "alley," but a "thoroughfare." The next day the assistant pastor said, "You're a strange duck," referring to the fact that I had dared to confront the monsignor. Ever after, when the monsignor came to the convent with ice cream for some special occasion, he made it a point to single me out and ask about my family.

Once, when the monsignor was ill in the hospital, he called one of the nuns to ask her to pick up some steaks for—and his voice trailed off. She anticipated him saying "for the nuns," but he ended his sentence with "for my dog." This same monsignor refused parish membership to a Black family. I was aghast.

In winter we wore long, black, heavy woolen mantles which elicited name calling of "crows" by eighth grade boys, followed by "Caw, caw!" At first I thought it disrespectful, but later, considering the mentality of the source, I had to admit it was rather funny. Some young boys referred to us as "Mrs. Zorro." Once a young child stared at me and then asked her mother, "Is that Mrs. God?"

Long before recycling became a nationwide habit, Milwaukee required that household garbage be separated from metal and glass containers. After each meal, we neatly wrapped our garbage in a few sheets of newspaper in the style of a butcher wrapping a piece of meat. Plastic bags were not common, so this method worked well to prevent leakage and odors.

Twice a year the Catholic Boy Scouts held paper drives to raise funds for their troops. On a designated Saturday morning parishioners who had saved up newspapers for recycling brought them to a huge van parked on the school playground. Computers had not yet become common household appliances and almost everyone read at least one newspaper a day.

The clergy bought roller skates for the nuns to use in the school gym. Since the gym doubled as a ballroom for parish fundraisers, a multi-faceted, mirrored disco ball hung from the ceiling, and as it revolved it cast flecks of light to the far reaches of the room. I loved it. If I had no courses to attend after school I went to the gym, put on an LP of Herb Alpert's Tijuana Brass, and skated to my heart's content, tapping the terrazzo floor to the tempo of "The Spanish Flea."

The school had two janitors, as they were then called, who were displaced persons from World War II and were sometimes referred to as "D.P.'s." One of them was shell-shocked and though able to perform his duties, was observably upset and could barely speak coherently. The other sometimes shot pigeons off the school roof early on Saturday mornings, and by 5 a.m. could be seen vacuuming the feathers off the lawn.

It was during this time that I had my first artwork published. It was for the Polish version of a religious publication called *The Franciscan Message* (*Kalendarz Franciszkański*) for the years 1968 and 1969. I illustrated twenty-four calendar mastheads for two years and received a check for $50, which in keeping with the vow of poverty, I dutifully submitted to the superior. No mention was made of what to me was a thrilling achievement.

Even though I had taught in five different towns during my ten years of teaching, I had not experienced much of them because we were not allowed to leave the house except out of necessity. This was not true in Milwaukee. A well-respected family in the parish invited me to their home for brunch or dinner on Sunday about once a month. I requested and always received permission to accept the invitation. By that time I had taken perpetual vows, was fully professed, and was therefore granted more privileges.

During these social occasions I was introduced to "Scarlet O'Hara" and "Bloody Mary" cocktails. The visit began in the early afternoon and included tours of various points of interest in the city, including the Mitchell Park Horticulture Conservatory, known as "The Domes." And on my twenty-seventh birthday these friends took me to dinner at the famed Pfister Hotel. When we ordered drinks, the waitress asked me, "Pardon me, Ma'am, but are you of age?"

I was sacristan again. Since there were five clergy at this large parish we now put out as many sets of vestments, cleaned and polished an equal number of chalices, and tided up after five Masses. In addition to classroom teaching, I spent a lot of time cleaning and decorating for the Christmas and Easter celebrations. After Christmas Midnight Mass, two of us sat in the sacristy, exhausted. Quietly, one

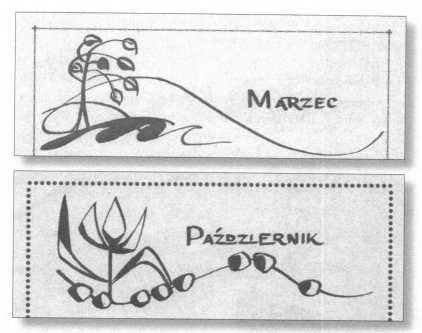

Mastheads for March depicting wind and for October, the month of the holy rosary.

of the assistant pastors came in, gave us a bottle of wine, thanked us for all our work, and left. This was an unusual gesture of appreciation. We invited a third nun to join us and stayed in the sacristy to enjoy the wine, but never told the superior. Similarly, Easter required special preparations for Holy Thursday and Good Friday as well as cleaning up well after midnight on Holy Saturday.

During this year the effects of Vatican II began to filter through the order's hierarchy. As a result, we were allowed to wear a modified veil, raise the hem of our habit to six inches off the ground (doubling the previous limit of three) and got rid of the wimple. I was glad because mine never fit well and irritated my throat. We were also allowed to wear secular clothes for casual wear. "Casual" meant cleaning the convent, sacristy, and sanctuary. One of the middle-aged nuns chided me for being the first to modify my habit.

It was around this time that I was invited to participate in a fashion show in Chicago. One of the sisters on our mission had a sister who was a fashion designer whose final project for graduation was to design modified habits for nuns.

At the end of the school year, the Provincial Mother called me out of my classroom to ask me to become school principal in Oshkosh. I felt honored and terrified simultaneously. I credit the convent for recognizing leadership qualities I didn't know I had. There was

no preparatory training for this administrative position. After eight years of teaching, I had recently earned the now seemingly redundant Bachelor of Science Degree in Education, with honors. This was considered adequate qualification. By this time, I had given up on the idea of ever becoming an artist.

In the fall of 1969, at the age of twenty-seven, I became a teaching principal at St. Josephat Parish in Oshkosh, Wisconsin. During this time many students at universities were protesting the Vietnam War,

In modified habit after Vatican II Council, 1968.

but not at the state university in Oshkosh. Here the students shut down a street to protest the beer drinking age. If they were old enough to be drafted at age eighteen, surely they should be allowed to drink at that age instead of twenty-one.

I managed the school, hired staff, and taught all subjects for forty-five rowdy seventh and eighth graders. They ran back and forth on the roof of our one-story building. Beneath the carpet in the entry, they found the opening to the crawl space under the building and disappeared. My students boasted of how they had intimidated previous lay teachers: "How come you're never sick on Monday mornings? One teacher was always sick on Mondays and didn't show up. Another would run out of the classroom crying. One teacher got pregnant, but that wasn't our fault." I listened. It was nice to be briefed on what to expect. The staff and I established policy. With the

On the far right, I participate in modeling new designs for nuns' habits.

pastor's hearty approval, we hand-delivered report cards to the parents at each child's home. The school changed overnight. Both parents and students were delighted we took such personal interest in them.

Once there was a slight relapse in behavior. My students came in from recess and as they sat down, they continuously stomped their feet in unison. I let them, noting the time. In a little while they began to peter out. I said, "Oh, come on, you can do better than that." The brighter students knew something was up and stopped while the rest continued. I noted the time again. The wasted time was deducted from their next recess. Action trumped verbal reprimand and they never tried that again.

At the end of the school year, I refused to take the still somewhat unruly eighth graders on a class trip to the Milwaukee Zoo, as was the custom. When the parents objected, I suggested they take them on the trip. They did. When they returned they said they would never do it again.

The following year we were transferred out because of the shortage of nuns, and the school was closed. Later, the president of the school board requested our return and offered to pay a lay teacher's salary which was highly unusual, but many nuns had begun to leave the order and there just weren't enough to go around. It was a sign of the times in religious orders. Nevertheless, it was gratifying to receive the request.

I spent the next two years teaching fifth and sixth graders back at Stevens Point, at St. Peter's Parish. It was heaven. The subjects were easy; the children superbly behaved. I had the added responsibility of teaching altar boys to recite parts of the Mass in Latin.

As more Sisters left the convent, the pastor had to hire additional lay teachers at a higher salary. He said of us, "They bite the hand that feeds them." At $2,000 a year per Sister, the major portion of which was sent to the motherhouse for operating expenses and the care of aged sisters, we had become cheap labor. Although we received housing, the clergy received not only housing but board, a secretary, a housekeeper, and a considerably higher salary, not to mention adulation. Thoreau said it best: "He who gives himself entirely to his fellow-men appears to them useless and selfish; but he who gives himself partially to them is pronounced a benefactor and philanthropist."

An accurate description of our lives is found in Margaret McGuinness' book *Called to Serve, A History of Nuns in America*. She writes: "Women religious received only one-half the salary of religious brothers, who receive half the salary of public school teachers. Most were inadequately educated and took 15 or more years to complete their education which they pursued after school, on Saturdays and during the summer. Because lay teachers required a higher salary, many of the sisters taught in overcrowded classrooms."

DURING THIS TIME, AS the order was relaxing its regulations, we were given a $30 a month allowance for personal spending. This was to cover postage, long distance phone calls, clothing, travel, and incidentals. Driving was no longer restricted, so I signed up for private driving instruction, using my entire monthly allowance. So it was, that at the age of thirty I finally acquired a driver's license.

But I was getting bored. In nine years, I had taught all the grades

November 22, 1970

Sister Theresa
St. Peters
800 4th St.
Stevens Point, Wisc.

Dear Sister,

It has just been brought to my attention that starting next school term the staffing of schools will be changed so that there will be a chance for selection by the teacher of the school of her choice.

We were very happy with the results brought about last term when you, Sister Jean, and Sister Elizabeth were here at St Josephs. I also realize that we would only be allowed a maximum of two Sisters, but wonder if we could contract for two of you and hire the third as a lay teacher with the salary of a lay teacher which could be used as you saw fit.

I would appreciate if you would talk this over with the other sisters and consider whether or not this would be possible. Please contact me and advise me if a meeting would be of value. If I knew enough in advance, I would arrange to meet you in Stevens Point and discuss the matter further.

Sincerely,

Donald L. Gerth
1600 Algoma Blvd.
Oshkosh, Wisc. 54901

Letter requesting our return to teach at this parish.

and been school principal. It was time for a change. I became Religious Education Coordinator at Resurrection Parish in Green Bay and worked with a wonderful Sister who shared the title. Even though we directed the program, we never held the title but were always called coordinators.

We solicited and trained volunteers to teach religion classes for almost a thousand public school preschool, elementary, and high school students in the evenings and on Saturdays. We designed programs, planned schedules, coordinated activities, and solved disciplinary problems. We held special classes and retreat weekends for teenagers and adults, planned liturgies, celebrations and parish events. In addition, I taught seventh grade religion classes and acted as religious consultant to the day staff at the parochial school. It was a progressive and upscale parish with an avant-garde pastor. Although we worked twelve-hour days, it was stimulating and rewarding.

We no longer had a cook, so we took turns preparing meals. It wasn't difficult, except there wasn't much time to do it—usually an hour. I was often overly ambitious with the desserts and once made

Baked Alaska, which took almost as long to prepare as the rest of the meal. We felt appreciated by the pastor as well as the parishioners, but again I became restless.

The Church was now emphasizing social justice, and I began to think it more appropriate to serve a needier segment of society. I also knew that I would not stay in the convent much longer and wanted to work with the impoverished before I left. After the school year ended, I left for Louisiana to work for social justice, known in the order as the "Social Apostolate." There I had experiences I could never have anticipated.

2

Four Years in the Deep South

Having read Paulo Friere's *Pedagogy of the Oppressed* among other books on disenfranchised segments of society, I decided in 1973 to volunteer at Saint Lucy Community Center located in the small town of Houma, Louisiana. I was tired of pious words and wanted to do something practical about poverty. Those were the days when we believed we could do anything; the harder, the better. In addition, I knew I would leave the order and wanted to work with the impoverished before I left. I was ready for adventure.

In this humid subtropical climate everything that grew blossomed at one time or another; crepe myrtle, camellias, gardenias, magnolias. Red roses climbed well into December, and in March the azaleas burst into color. The floating water hyacinths layered the bayous with lavender loveliness. Later I learned they were an invasive species that suffocated aquatic life beneath, alligators being excepted. Another invasive species was the kudzu vine which eerily covered the trees, telephone poles and almost any fixed object.

I liked the South. The people, like the climate, were warm. If a friend was invited to a party, it was assumed they could bring along a guest, even if unknown to the host. This was unheard of in the part of the north with which I was familiar. Shrimp was fifty cents a pound off the boat. And oh, the mockingbird! If interrupted, it continued where it left off till it got to the bottom of the page. Every day in summer, predictably at 4 p.m., the moisture came in on the Gulf sea breeze with a downpour not unlike the Morton Salt slogan of "When it Rains, it Pours." The image of the girl with the umbrella always came to mind. Although the rain was so heavy one could not drive in it, it was short lived.

Birds chorused mercilessly every morning at 4 a.m. The temperature all summer long was 90 degrees with 90 percent humidity. It was a mercy we had air conditioning in some of the rooms at the community center where we lived and worked. We each had private rooms on the second floor, while the first floor held offices, dining and living rooms, a kitchen and a lovely screened back porch. Chameleons darted playfully over the screens. The director of the community center lived in a separate building, but joined us for meals.

The staff included the founder and principal of the Montessori Day Care from Missouri, the cook from Pennsylvania, and me, the Homestart coordinator. There was also a social worker who became chagrined when I learned my job too quickly. She who was from Ireland, told me to go back to Wisconsin where I belonged! Since I was not living with sisters of my own order I had to handle my own finances. At the age of thirty, I learned how to open a bank account and write a check. Because I was working on a voluntary basis, I received a stipend from the provincial home for food and personal needs. Out of the spirit of poverty I asked for only $130 a month.

The community center operated under the auspices of the Archdiocese of New Orleans, as a part of its social apostolate program. Its primary purpose was to provide education for preschoolers, and secondarily to refer other observed problems to the Terrebonne Parish Social Service department. The name "Terrebonne" translates as "Good Earth." The community center was not government funded but supported by the Archdiocese, private donors, grants and parents who could afford to pay something.

Its focal point was the Montessori Day Care which, incidentally, Maria Montessori originated for the purpose of serving the very poor and not as it has since become, a school for children of middle class and upscale families. Our day care principal, a certified Montessori instructor had trained ten local African-American women to become

(above) Children from the Montessori Day Care boarding the bus.

(below) Visitors from the north in front of my first attempt at sign painting: 'St. Lucy's Montessori Children's House.'

qualified Montessori instructors who held certificates from England. This generated much pride among the women and the community. The objective was to make the school self-sufficient and for the principal to work herself out of a position.

My primary functions were to serve as Homestart Coordinator, not to be confused with Headstart, the government agency, and Home Visitor. I received referrals to the program from the overflow of applicants to the Montessori Day Care as well as from Terrebonne Parish's social services department. Sometimes the families I visited referred me to additional families. At other times, neighbor children simply showed up.

On my way to teach children in their homes—believing that I could make a difference.

In a car without air conditioning, I visited as many as five homes a day to teach preschool Homestart classes to fifty children a week. I taught classes in reading and math readiness and trained the mother to educate her child. In most cases, I merely needed to build the confidence of the mother and to supply her with homemade teaching materials and she was happy to teach her child. The idea was to prepare children so they would not fail in first grade, given there were no free public school kindergartens available to this segment of society. This would not be so terrible for children of normal middle class homes. I myself had not attended kindergarten, but these children lived in extremely deprived circumstances.

I carried with me books, flashcards and other materials along with a small phonograph which I used to accompany singing and physical exercises. Grade school children I had taught at St. Stanislaus School in Stevens Point, sent donations for school supplies. As a follow-up, I always left behind a small written exercise, prestigiously referred to as "homework." More often than not, as I knocked on the door the following week, the homework was lying in the mud under the door stoop. It made me appreciate the desks we had when I was growing up, desks configured with orange crates standing on end with a spare dining table leaf over them. At least we had a place to put our stuff, where no sibling dared touch it.

Nor was there a place for the adults to store important papers except between the mattress and bed springs. I had read of this but was astonished to see it firsthand. That is where the mother stored the birth certificates of her children, if there was a birth certificate. Some of the children had trouble getting into first grade because they could not produce the certificate. If they were born in the ambulance on its way to Charity Hospital in New Orleans, the attendants sometimes forgot to register the birth. Another obstacle was to obtain transportation to register their children for first grade.

The secondary objective of Homestart was to learn the needs of families and to coordinate efforts with other agencies to try to improve their living situations. I tried hard not to come across as a patronizing northerner trying to fix the South. I visited the homes of Native Americans, African-Americans and Caucasians. The common denominator was dire poverty. I detected no prejudice among these multi-ethnic families. They were all struggling to survive.

In this town of Houma, with just over 9,000 dwellings, there were over 500 homes with inadequate plumbing and 250 without hot water. The community center staff approached the City for the housing ordinance which they said they were unable to locate. Later we learned that if the inspector identified the problem in any particular ward, he was liable to lose his job because the landlords would file false complaints against him. In one home the family bought and had installed their own water heater, only to have the rent raised because the improvement would raise taxes for the landlord.

We confronted City Hall about the hot water problem only to learn that some of the largest contributing benefactors of our community center were on the City Council. They threatened to cut off their contributions if we raised a fuss: a lesson in politics. We

Home visiting with three families at this house.

had reports and photographs published in the newspaper. Nothing changed. If a tenant filed a complaint, that tenant risked eviction. I realized if I were to make a difference, it would be on a one-to-one basis on a personal level, inspiring people to make small changes in their own lives. It seemed to be about all I could do.

Sometimes three families lived in two rooms to consolidate resources. The homes did not smell good and were infested with cockroaches and sometimes rats. By the time I got back to my car, my feet jumped with fleas. When I read the story of "*101 Dalmatians*" by Dodie Smith, a preschooler looked at the illustrations and declared, "That dog have fleas!" Often while I read to the preschoolers, they stroked my hair and commented on its smoothness when all the while I thought they were concentrating on the story. One child asked if I had a husband, and barring that, did I have a grandmother? When I sat down to teach in a home, I usually headed for vinyl-covered furniture which was less likely to harbor roaches or fleas. Once when I plopped myself down on a vinyl-covered couch, I found myself in a puddle of urine from a child who had slept there the previous night. After rushing home to take a shower, I returned to teach the lesson. I hoped I was providing an example of not letting obstacles obstruct objectives.

(left) Having fun finger painting with a small friend. (right) Matching colors during Homestart. In the background, a student strays from the program.

Some of the mothers thought their children were not capable of learning anything until they reached the magic age of six and were surprised at their preschool progress. Others said, "Ever since you been coming, the children be so bad." I took this as a compliment since it meant their minds had been stimulated, and they were no longer satisfied with doing nothing.

The children as well as their mothers eagerly anticipated my arrival. I was amazed that they so willingly let me into their homes. It seemed like a breach of privacy. But wearing the veil gave me credibility. I think I was the only outside visitor they had besides the occasional funeral insurance agent. In one home the mother so looked forward to my weekly Tuesday visit that she always washed the floor so I could teach on it. There seldom were tables, and I did not want to teach on a bed. In other homes, the roaches sometimes scurried over the flashcards I placed on the floor. A child would slap them away, shouting, "Go, roach!"

Stoves had ovens that did not work and were covered with decorative contact paper. I was impressed with the ingenuity of these people. No drain plug? Stuff it with a washcloth. No dryer? Hang the clothes above the stove burners. No hammer? Pound in the nail with the heel of a shoe. Incidentally, there was no sheetrock in the interior of these houses. The wood siding I saw on the outside was the same I saw on the inside. Once when I visited a woman in one of these

Teaching Homestart class on the front porch.

homes, she proudly stated that her four sons now lived in Chicago and had obtained college degrees.

Except in rare instances, I am not an advocate of donating food; it seems to assuage one's conscience without getting involved with people who need dedicated help to develop resources to buy their own food. But in an effort to involve myself with the broader community and to develop a connection between the haves and have nots, I delivered turkeys with the Junior League before Christmas. The next day some of the volunteers went to check on these families only to be disappointed to see the children playing with the turkey, dragging it around in the yard. "How ungrateful," was their response. I later learned neither the stove nor refrigerator worked in the home. It was tough to try to get to the bottom of a problem, and even then there wasn't much that could be done about it. All the good will in the world can be useless if not well informed.

I also taught in the "projects," as they were called then. It was public housing for those on welfare. Our director cautioned against us going alone, but I went during the day when it was safest. I was too impatient to try to coordinate with the other staff member. Often there was a pipe-smoking grandmother on the front porch who warned me away if there was a male in the house. Most of the houses were occupied by mothers and children.

As I visited homes, I noticed a ten-year-old boy who had a wound so deep on the top of his foot the bone was exposed. Since the children played in a muddy alley with broken glass, I feared gangrene would set in and insisted on taking him and his mother to the doctor only to learn the doctor recommended soaking the child's foot in Epsom salts. The doctor's fee was $30, the exact welfare amount the family received for the month. I felt like a do-gooder who needed to learn a lesson. A year later, the boy saw me in the yard at the community center. "Do you remember me?" he asked. I didn't. "I'm the boy you took to the doctor when I had a cut on my foot." He showed me his completely healed foot, thanked me, and smiled broadly.

During another home visit, I saw severely developmentally and physically disabled six-month-old Aletha lying immobile on a bed with flies walking over her face. This child eventually showed up at the children's home where I worked later. Four-year-old Regina was so hungry she ate grass; handfuls of it, not just a blade to chew on as children sometimes do. Later we were able to get her into the Montessori Day Care where she received at least two meals a day. There was also a home where a three-year-old cared for a one-year-old all day while the mother worked. I could not believe these conditions could exist in this country as late as 1974. Years later, when I worked at a community employment agency in Minneapolis, Minnesota, I noted that child care, particularly sick child care, was the largest obstacle for single mothers trying to get off welfare to work.

I encountered an unusual testament to segregation when I went to teach in a home on Jessamine Street. There, crossing the street at a right angle to it, was a tall palisade fence. On one side of it lived the white people, and on the other lived the Black people, cut off from one another.

Field trips for preschool children included riding the elevator and escalator at the mall. This was a first for the children and an opportunity for me to teach good manners in public. I heard a clerk say, "Not her again!" I thought that was funny. I took them to grocery stores to teach names of fruit and vegetables and to not touch. Sometimes I took photographs and sent them to the local newspaper with a little write-up. It was good publicity for our community center and not only encouraged donations but augmented the pride of the family whose child appeared in the photo. I made it a habit to obtain an extra copy for the respective parent. The groups were very small and I tried to include a mother whenever possible to get her out of the house, too.

A trip to the grocery store to reinforce a Homestart lesson. (Courtesy *Houma Daily Courier)*

Another reason for inviting a mother along was to demonstrate there was another way of getting children to behave besides yelling at them. One day on a trip to the park, a child threw a candy wrapper out the window. I stopped the car right there and we got out to retrieve the wrapper. The children were surprised and had never heard of such a thing as littering being unacceptable.

Besides Homestart and Home Visiting, I organized and taught summer day camp for older children at the community center. I trained instructors and volunteers, taught adult evening classes in ceramics, planned talent nights and participated in fundraising events for our center, all in the aforementioned hot and humid conditions.

Field trips for older children in day camp included a trip to Baton Rouge to visit the state capitol. They were thrilled to look out the top of the tower. No one ever saw a better behaved group of children. For many of them, it was their first trip outside their small town. Another field trip involved taking them to the still segregated swimming pool. Based on my observation of the sleeve lines on their arms, I noticed Black children got suntans, too. When they scraped an elbow or a knee, they were as pink as a white person beneath a very thin layer of pigment. It was then that I noted Band-aids came only in Caucasian flesh tones. No one thought to make Black Band-aids, though today they come in colors and designs completely alien to anyone's skin tones.

This work had its enter-taining moments. Once when the rain came through the roof while I was teaching remedial math and reading in summer day camp, a child warned, "Careful, teacher, you'll get a wrinkle in your hair." A small girl observed my tall, thin stature and mimicked a likely adult remark, "You're getting big, aren't you?" Another not-ed the wrinkles in my cotton clothing in no uncertain terms: "I can tell you sat in *that* skirt!"

Taking the Homestart children for an outing in the park in May. A mother in the background looks on.

The children were most affectionate. A fourth-grade boy thought nothing of leaning against me as I sat at my desk prompting him with his reading. When I had taught in the North, a child that age wouldn't be caught dead leaning against his teacher for fear of being dubbed "teacher's pet." Another time, a classroom with walls and ceiling painted black seemed to make the hot, windowless room close in on us. A small boy, who could hardly stand it, stared at the clock as it neared dismissal time and burst out, "Bell, why don't you ring yourself!"

One day, one of our children at the day care was struck by a car and decapitated. Our staff was invited to the Black Baptist funeral services for the child. I felt privileged to be invited. It was an other-worldly experience for me. Four women dressed in white and wearing nurses' caps fanned the mourning mother. The preacher and choir became more and more intense in their songs and prayers to the point where the mourner fainted, became rigid and was carried out in full length by the women.

Our 69-year-old cook was raped early one morning as she walked to church for 5 a.m. Mass. When I came down for breakfast, she was sitting alone in the dining room. The rest of the staff had left for vacation this particular week. She had hailed a passing police car immediately after the incident, but they took off in the direction the rapist had fled, leaving her where she was. She walked the remainder of the distance to the church, attended the service and then asked a parishioner to take her home. I was furious at the police for abandoning her where she had been raped. I took her to the doctor, brought her back home to the community center, and then went to the police to give them a piece of my mind. I learned that the cook had used the word "attacked" instead of "raped", hence the misunderstanding. Women of her era were uncomfortable using the more accurate term.

Back at the community center, I spoke with reporters and investigators. Later the account appeared on the front page of the local newspaper. The Blacks in the community were outraged. They highly revered this woman because she was the sister of the priest who established the first high school for Blacks in town in 1956 when they were not allowed to attend public high schools. This later became St. Lucy Community Center. I remembered that was the year I had started high school. Later I took her to the police station to identify the suspects in the line-up. I thought she recognized one, but she insisted she recognized none of them. I thought she might be protecting the clientele her priest brother had served for so many years, but one can never get inside another person's mind. The *Houma Daily Courier* carried two front page stories on the incident.

The director of our community center, who lived in the former pastor's rectory, had a niece with seven children living in the state. He invited me to join his family for an outing at Grand Isle on the Gulf Shore. At the first meeting of the children, they were immediately affectionate toward me and to my surprise, kissed me on the lips. We stayed at a camp on stilts near the sea. It was wonderful. I learned to catch, purge and boil crabs: "First, you tie a turkey neck to the inside of the bottom of the net...."

To purge the crabs, we put them in a large container and poured salt over them so they regurgitated silt. Finally, a large pot with potatoes was brought to a boil and Zatarain's seasoning and lemons added. The live crabs were tossed into the boiling water. After 20 minutes, the crabs and potatoes were spilled out on a table covered with newspaper and served with beer. At night the rhythm of the waves lulled me to sleep. It was an unforgettable sound and I can call up the memory of it still. I slept slack-jawed for eleven hours.

On another occasion, Archbishop Philip Hannan of New Orleans came down to visit our community center. He was very ordinary and easy to talk to, and wanted to hear about our work. During World War II, he was commissioned in the United States Army, where he served as a chaplain to the 82nd Airborne Division. Joining the 82nd in Belgium, he ministered to the paratroopers during the Ardennes Offensive. He marveled at how the Poles were fearless in parachute assault operations. Afterward he took the staff to the Gulf Shore for an outing. His dignity was such that it was not impaired when he swam with us in the Gulf. Because of the saltwater it was easy to stay afloat. So now I can say I went swimming with the Archbishop.

In 1974 Hurricane Carmen hit the Gulf Coast, which included Louisiana. Part of our staff volunteered with the Red Cross at Cocodrie, a fishing, shrimping, and crabbing village on the very southern edge of the state. We mostly filled out purchase agreements for the victims, many of whom came in their pirogues. Cocodrie feels like the end of the world. In fact, if you drive down Highway 56 through it, you will first encounter watery areas across the road and then end up in the Gulf itself!

Nuns in New Orleans always got free bus rides. This was in gratitude for their devoted service during Hurricane Betsy in 1965. The southerners seemed to appreciate the Sisters and the work they did. I did not hear negative remarks or silly jokes about them.

71

During this time I met a group of women artists called The Red Geranium who invited me to participate in their art exhibits. This was fun and a learning experience for me. We sent out invitations and held exhibitions at the Magnolia House, an antebellum home, the Southland Mall, and at Holy Rosary convent where I lived after leaving St. Lucy's Community Center. It was the first time I sold some paintings, for which I received recognition from the motherhouse and provincial home.

After my two years at the community center, a free public school kindergarten opened to include minorities. The Montessori Day Care became independent of its principal a year earlier, who then left, her mission fulfilled. The director found employment in another state, and I found a position at MacDonell Children's Services, located in the same town.

"WINTERWONDERLAND" is this year's theme for the annual Christmas show sponsored by the Red Geranium Artists. Shown planning the display are Rita Mae Hoffman, Sister Terry Wanta and Betty Grummer. Everyone is invited to browse through "Winterwonderland" at Southland Mall Dec. 2-7.

Announcement of our show in the *Houma Daily Courier.*

I applied for the position of Case Manager Assistant at the children's home that was privately operated by a Methodist religious group. In those halcyon days, I was promoted to Supervisor of the Emergency Care Receiving Unit during the interview. This doesn't happen anymore despite my improved competence. During the interview, the director of the home asked what I would do if a child climbed onto the roof and threatened to jump off. At that time I thought it a trick question.

This was an emergency care receiving unit for abused and neglected children who had been removed from their homes. My job was to provide for physical, medical, social and educational needs of

One of our exhibits was held at Magnolia House.

the children as well as to hire and supervise an assistant and four aides. I was offered $10,000 a year in 1975, and was tempted to withhold it from the motherhouse. I planned to leave the order after my time there and knew the motherhouse wouldn't know the difference because my previous work had been done on a voluntary basis. But integrity prevailed. I was still under the vow of poverty and dutifully submitted the paychecks. After I left the order, I gave the lie to my integrity because I regretted not keeping the money. Integrity did not pay the rent.

The Receiving Unit was an experimental project at the children's home. It was located on the second floor of a white, high ceilinged plantation style building situated among magnificent ancient Water Oaks with gnarled branches that sprawled endlessly. The dining room and kitchen on the first floor served dinner for our unit plus six additional permanent foster care units on campus. Those six units housed school age children who had failed in private foster homes. Our Receiving Unit was the only one that received infants and the only one that housed children on a temporary basis prior to placement in foster care.

The children in our un-airconditioned building ranged in age from two months through 16 years. I was on duty for four 24-hour days alternating with my assistant who worked the remaining three days. The four aides each worked eight hour shifts around the clock because of the precarious condition of the children. I slept the night shift in an apartment attached to the unit. After a day spent dealing with tapeworms, ear infections, heat rash and emotional outbursts (of staff and children) I dutifully dictated case notes on each child before dropping into bed. Often the aide fell asleep while on night duty. After I dismissed one negligent employee, her son called me late at night with death threats. When I immediately called the director, he told me not to bother him and that my call had disturbed his wife.

Some of the children came to us directly from the hospital, others were referred by Social Services, but all were from abusive and negligent homes. I recognized some from the homes I visited previously when I had worked at the community center. They were undernourished, out-rightly tortured and predictably angry. It is one thing to read about abused children and quite another to hold one in your arms, covered with scars.

The sixteen-year old love child of a prostitute, whose mother found it too troublesome to care for at this age, joined our motley family at the unit. He seemed to do well until one day his roommate came running to me, relating breathlessly that the newcomer was on the roof. Here was the truth of what I had supposed was a trick question asked of me during the interview. I told the youngster to join the other children. I didn't need an audience for this. To the boy on the roof I repeated what I had said to the director during the interview: "Come down off the roof. I don't want you to hurt yourself, but I can't wait here any longer because the little babies need me." After a few minutes, there he was, joining us in the other room. Whew!

For two years I experienced vicarious motherhood in this unit. A one-year-old arrived who would not allow us to touch him but remained in a fetal position, sucking his thumb. It was nearly impossible to feed him, bathe him and change his diaper. After a number of months he became a sassy little boy; laughing, running around and teasing other children. In fact, he thought it was fun to bite them! One child was so accustomed to abuse she did not even cry when his bite broke the skin on her arm. I remember the first time I gave him a spoon to feed himself. How many times did he load the spoon and promptly miss his mouth, landing the food in his hair?

All I could think of was that somewhere his mother was missing this milestone in his progress while I got to enjoy it.

I held in my arms two-year-old Anthony who had cigarette burns everywhere on his body but the soles of his feet. The first words spoken by this child of gentle disposition were "F--- you." He rather sang it, without the usual inflection we may be accustomed to hearing. Another child of the same age had a foreign object removed from her vagina when she came to us from the hospital. Three-year-old Regina had scars on her cheek from table fork punctures and referred to each staff member as "bitch." Her pelvis was broken at six months when she had been thrown against the wall. When she and her sister were removed from their home, the mother threatened to have another child. The problem was the mother often had a child "to have someone to love her." And so it was that mothers themselves were children.

Two-year-old Stacy had an infected area two inches in diameter on the back of her head when she arrived. It was filled with pus, and the hair had fallen out. The aides were very good at dealing with these children. After the wound had healed, it was gratifying to have her announce proudly that she had "washed her hands, flushed the toilet and shut the door." We hoped not in that order.

The police brought us a fourteen-year-old from the bayous who was a victim of incest by her father and from whom she had contracted a venereal disease. To escape him, she had herself put in jail. The mother had died some years ago, and both her older sisters had satisfied his needs until they left home. The night the girl spent in jail, the father deliberately but carefully shot himself in the foot, blaming her for "making him do that to himself." The girl's sisters also blamed her for their father's injury. They were angry at this youngest sister because if they had to go through the ordeal, why shouldn't she?

The assistant director who procured supplies complained that I was too demanding. I had returned canned fruit juice meant for the babies that was so old the acid had eaten through the lids. I wanted a dustpan to pick up the dirt. I reported it was so hot in the unit the milk soured in the refrigerator. To this he asked if it was plugged in.

The staff had the last laugh when this assistant director substituted for the cook one weekend while she was on vacation. The chicken, mashed potatoes and green beans were all seasoned with the same barbecue sauce, casting an orange pall over the meal. Best of all, the package of giblets was still inside the roasted chicken! We never stopped regaling the cook with the incident upon her return.

I acquired a chauffeur's license to drive a small bus to transport the children to doctor appointments, to spend their small allowances and take them on outings. We had no child safety seats, and there were no extra staff to spare. When I had to take a two-month-old to the doctor, I put her in a cardboard box lined with blankets and placed it near me on the floor of the bus. When I took a group of children of various ages, races and colors to spend their allowances downtown, passersby remarked "What a weird-looking family!" I found this amusing. I was proud of my little family.

One of our children who was half Native American asked, "Which way am I half Indian? This way or that way?" motioning vertically and horizontally on himself. Five-year-old Steven said to me, "Teacher, you a honky." "What?" I said, not familiar with the term. "Let's go outside and play," he quickly evaded. They often referred to me as "teacher" since that was the only capacity in which they regularly interacted with whites.

Once there was a fire at 2 a.m. in our unit. As luck would have it, the aide had not shown up for her night shift. I got up every two hours to check on the five children in the unit. Four were under the age of two and one was five. As I saw smoke near the ceiling in the hallway, I wondered if I were dreaming. I wasn't. I took the children downstairs, two at a time, one under each arm and called the fire department. This was before the 911 code, so emergency numbers were listed near the phone. The fire department number was one digit off, so I had to look it up in the telephone directory.

I then reported the fire to the director who lived on the premises. He said he would care for the children outside while I should run back up into the building for the key to unlock the back gate for fire truck access. Having been schooled in obedience and since there were no visible flames yet, I, in my lavender flannel nightgown with the ruffle on the bottom, ran back into the building. It is absurd to remember the detail of the ruffle, but sometimes during a crisis, one remembers the most insignificant things.

The fire had started under the landings at the ends of the stairwells where unbelievably, there were gas jets to heat our building on colder nights. Because the temperature had dropped to 35 degrees above zero that night, the city boosted the gas pressure which caused the flames to reach the floorboards above.

I did not sleep the remainder of the night. I took care of the next two shifts since it was Thursday, the crossover day, when no aides were scheduled. It was also laundry day for my unit, so I did that, too, lugging the laundry baskets up the steep stairs. All the director had to say was, "Too bad you didn't let it burn down, we could have collected the insurance."

Again, I was surprised this could be happening in this country and at the late date of 1977. Near the end of these two years, I had steeled myself against my feelings for these children and began to bathe and feed them systematically, forgetting to hug them, talk to them and stroke their heads. I knew then that it was time to leave. The strange thing was, I never panicked during any of these emergencies. That happened many years later when I worked under tight deadlines at a major corporation. A year after I left, I was taken aback when the director of the children's home called me in Wisconsin and asked if I would consider returning to the position I had previously held there.

At the end of my four years in Louisiana I had an incomparable feeling of satisfaction. I had learned more than I taught, and received far more than I had given. While I realized my experience reflected only one portion of one town in one state, I wished every citizen in this country were compelled to at least two years of service with the impoverished. Surely this would bridge the gap of misunderstanding. White people had misconceptions of Black people, and the Blacks had understandable prejudices against the whites. It would help to understand that all white people are not alike, nor are all Black people alike. I also wished that people not be allowed to have children unless they were trained, tested and licensed to be fully qualified as parents. After all, that is a requirement for driving inanimate vehicles.

To this day, I wonder what became of these children. They would be in their forties and fifties by now. It is easy to be understanding and compassionate toward children, but once they become adults, we expect them magically to become responsible citizens. After I returned to the North to pursue my long deferred degree in fine arts, it seemed strange to see children laughing and playing with carefree spirit. In church, people argued about which hymns should be sung at the liturgy. Didn't they know children were starving and beaten in this country at this moment? So it is that we expect others to have an understanding of things that only we have personally experienced.

Now I was ready to embark on my long deferred art career. Eventually this would mean I would leave religious life.

3

Oh, the Jobs I've Had!

I knew in my heart it was time to leave the convent. My transition from religious life to secular life was gradual. After the years in Louisiana, I returned to the provincial house in Stevens Point, Wisconsin and asked to obtain a bachelor's degree in fine art, my unfulfilled dream. The provincial mother agreed. While the courses were heaven on earth, I didn't feel right about having the order pay for my education when I knew I wouldn't be staying, and following a year of study I left the order.

Like a dutiful daughter of the Church, I wrote a letter to the pope to request a dispensation from my vows. It wasn't a difficult process and I experienced no resentment or ill will from the Provincial Mother or other sisters.

I remember being annoyed that the papal office couldn't even print out the entire blessing "And may God, etc." on the forms after all the years I had served. I was instructed to turn in my copies of the rule, constitution, and customs, as well as my 14k gold ring. I kept the gold ring for a bit of financial security. Although the order was obligated to return only the dowry of $50, I was given $500 to get started. This was generous, considering the order did not have much income. It was not a traumatic re-entry into secular life since I had already learned to use a checking account and knew how to drive, though there were adjustments to be made.

'Indult of Secularization' from the Holy See, front and back, in Latin.

I felt euphoric freedom, though I had no home, no job, and no car, savings, or credit. I lacked contacts and friends and did not own dishes, sheets, or even a salt shaker. I realized it had been my choice to enter the convent and my choice to leave. The deal was to work under the vow of poverty without remuneration, and I knew it when I signed on to that way of life. Nevertheless, I felt envy when I remembered a nun in Louisiana, who after leaving her order, was given a shower by the church parish where she worked to supply her with basic cooking utensils.

For $150 a month I rented a furnished apartment, (with a few dishes!). At age thirty-six, I did not qualify for a credit card because I had no financial history, while eighteen-year-old students were bombarded with credit card offers. As I searched for work, I realized I had worked on professional levels but did not want to divulge my religious background, suspecting that it would deter most employers from hiring me. So then how to account for all those years? No one would believe I had no money; it was a phrase used by those who didn't want to spend it. Besides, being single with no children, how could I not have any money at all at my age?

Stevens Point was a small city, and the three part-time jobs I eventually landed were low-paying, and totaled sixty hours a week, above and beyond the time I spent in class at the university. I calculated I was out of my apartment sixteen hours a day and paid rent only to sleep there. I spent $30 a month on groceries, always taking a sandwich with me to school and drinking free hot water in the cafeteria. Luckily, I received a PEO sisterhood grant through one of my instructors.

As a student at UW–Stevens Point, I found a part-time job as project assistant for a Native American HUD (Housing and Urban Development) program in the Education Department. I found another job working as a page at the public library. It was a CETA (Comprehensive Employment and Training Act) position designed for high school students. Since none applied, the library was happy to have an older, responsible person with a degree and a half. At the age of thirty-six, with sixteen years of professional experience, I was working for $2.60 an hour. But I still cherish friendships from that time.

My third job was to teach art to eight grades of children at a Catholic school where I had previously taught. I dreaded returning to that environment but did it until I found another part-time position as graphic designer in the News and Publications office at the university. There, through the kindness and patience of the assistant editor, I learned the trade from scratch. She and I remain friends today. To enhance my skills, I read every design book and magazine I could get my hands on. Often I ordered them through interlibrary loan services from as far away as Sarasota, Florida.

In the days before computers, layouts were keylined. That meant preparing an overlay for each color and taping them together in perfect registration. Overlays were done in rubylith, a thin red film that's carefully scored with an exacto knife into a shape and peeled off the underlying clear acetate, allowing for a different ink color for each layer. The design was usually 150 or 200 percent larger than the final product so that any imperfections would be reduced.

There was a shorthand code of instruction to indicate color, type style, size, spacing, and paragraph style. It reminded me of the markings left on trains and buildings by hobos. The vocabulary specific to the printing industry is somewhat masculine in tone: guts, bleeds, gutters, strippers. Other less colorful terms were "orphan" and "widow,"

My first printed brochure design as a graphic designer.

referring to a single word left on a line at the end of a paragraph. Eventually this job became a full-time academic staff position, and I dropped the others. I was pretty happy. I designed calendars, view books, departmental brochures, directories, and catalogs. It was rewarding to see my work in print. One of my summer catalog cover designs received a Wisconsin State Communications award.

In the months immediately after leaving the order, I tried things I had missed out on. I took horseback riding lessons, which caused my entire body to ache; I was no good at trying to control a horse. I tried ballet—something I had always dreamed of doing—but here again, every muscle became so sore that I soon quit. (Maybe the things we choose to pursue, to the exclusion of other things, reflect an unspoken, intuitive understanding of what we're likely to be good at.) I did buy a camera and cross country skis which I put to good use. Later, I bought roller skates, which I enjoyed using until I was in my seventies.

After a year, with a loan through the university credit union, I bought a used car and paid it off in six months. I couldn't believe my good fortune at obtaining a loan since I had just begun to work there. In addition to my design responsibilities, I supervised and trained student interns. An eighteen-year-old intern expressed envy that I, at the age of 38, owned a car! Another task I undertook was to observe and evaluate students in practice teaching for the Art Education Department. There was some irony in this.

In 1981, having tucked away a thousand dollars bit by bit, I took a trip to Russia through the International Programs Department at the university. I knew I should have saved the money, but I was playing "catch up" in my life and wanted very much to travel. Considered in retrospect, it was money well spent. That amount covered the flight, hotels, meals, and all interior travel for fifteen days. I had just finished a course in Russian art and architecture, which greatly enhanced my visit. I could identify and fully appreciate the palaces and church structures. The chapel in the Winter Palace, in then Leningrad, beautiful and unusual, was still in restoration from damage incurred during World War II. In the small town of Zagorsk, horses pulled sleighs. I dutifully read Hedrick Smith's first book, *Russia*, and found it right on target. I felt lucky to have been born in America by pure chance of the Ovarian Lottery. Warren Buffet states in his biography, which

In Moscow, 1981.

I read many years later, regarding some passing Chinese boatmen: "They were born there and destined to live there. They didn't have a chance. Pure luck that we were born in America. This is the Ovarian Lottery."

Back in Stevens Point I purchased a sleek pair of Bonna laminated wooden skis on sale for $89 (which I still have) and learned to cross-country ski, as much for the social as the physical engagement. New friends had invited me to join them for weekends at Telemark near Cable, Wisconsin. I enjoyed being accepted as a part of the group.

After wearing black and white clothing for twenty-two years, fashion went to my head. Usually the clothing I liked best was on the

After leaving the order, I developed a penchant for fashion.

sale rack because it was too avant garde for most people. I had fun trying out different looks.

In August, friends invited me to go canoeing in Quetico Provincial Park, in North Ontario. At this time, passports were not required, but to protect the park from litter, every non-organic object we had brought along was noted in writing at the park entry point, and we would be fined for each item that was missing when we exited the park. We were good stewards and left the park scot free.

On portages we two women carried fifty-pound backpacks containing food and supplies, while the four men carried the canoes and tents. Food included salami, pancake mix, new-fangled freeze-dried food developed on the space missions, and chocolate. Blueberries grew on some islands and provided a welcome fresh supplement to our food supply. As the days progressed, the packs got lighter while the salami became slightly rancid.

At forty, I was the oldest of the group; the youngest, an eighteen-year-old man, was a whiner. The three other men were seasoned Boy Scout leaders who had previously made numerous trips to this wilderness. They could navigate among the numerous islands and lakes, all of which looked alike to me. We had maps, just in case. We were glad they were printed on plastic, which was waterproof, but to our surprise and chagrin, the mosquito repellent on our hands began to smudge and dissolve the ink.

We admired Native American pictographs along the rocky island cliffs and caught one small bass, which we divided among ourselves in equal bites. The water was so pure we could see the bottom of the lake and drink directly from it, though we usually boiled it to be on the safe side. One evening after sundown, as we took a short canoe ride on a lake, one of the men could approximate the time by observing the stars. He based his judgement on the distance some constellations were from the horizon in the summer sky after locating the North Star by way of the Big Dipper.

The lakes we traversed included Sunday Lake, This Man Lake, That Man Lake, and Louisa Lake, famous for the magnificent Louisa Falls that gushed into it through the woods from the east. The flow of water was interrupted halfway in its descent by a large basin, which was not only sensational to see and hear, but to physically experience as we swam in the basin and felt the water crashing down around us before continuing to cascade to the lake.

We canoed for eight days with only one duff day when we sunned ourselves on the rocks and hung our hand-laundered clothing on the bushes. I developed strong biceps from doing the various strokes required to steer the craft and keep it moving. The minute the sun went down, the mosquitoes came out as if on cue. Safe in the mosquito-proof tent, we fell right to sleep, exhausted from the exercise and fresh air. An early riser, I peeked out of the tent one morning to find myself face to face with a moose. Before I could think, it blinked. Off into the woods it lumbered, out of sight of this relieved camper. But for the most part, all we saw on this trip were rocks, trees, sky, and water, then more water, sky, trees, and rocks. It was hard to go back to civilization, to come down from this high. I couldn't wait to get home to relive the experience in my imagination without the distraction of driving and merited a speeding ticket along the way.

That year, after designing an International Travel brochure on England, I decided to take the trip. At this time I had also begun to scout around to buy a house. But these were not to be. There were state budget cuts, and lacking seniority, I was laid off in December. Undaunted, I began to freelance in the tri-city area of Stevens Point, Wisconsin Rapids, and Marshfield, providing graphic design, illustration, and calligraphy services. By now I had graduated with a degree of Bachelor of Fine Arts, with honors.

One client expressed surprise that I could do such professional illustration "considering I was a woman." He actually said that. There were no free lancers in these small towns at the time, and so it was quite a new thing to see a woman doing this. In fact, there was at that time only one woman in town who owned her own business. When designing logos, I learned the image had to be versatile enough to be used on vehicles and buildings as well as on letterhead without compromising any of its elements. I learned to smile and network to obtain more leads. All in all, most people were supportive.

Two logos I designed on a freelance basis.

The Small Business Development Center at the university obtained several projects for me. I visited the university department heads with whom I had previously worked and asked for freelance projects. Even though my position had been cut, the needs would still be there. At holiday time I walked through the offices in my polyester navy blue suit with my leather briefcase to wish everyone a "Merry Christmas." One of the senior designers, ten years my junior, owned a house and apartments and still had his full-time job with benefits, expressed envy that I should be paid more per project than he was. Never mind my overhead expenses.

One of the department heads who had contracted my services and implemented my design called me after I moved to Minneapolis to ask if I would re-do the design in a different context. He was unwilling, however, to pay the modest fee I requested. Instead, he had a student copy the design from an old sample.

At 5 a.m., as the sun was barely rising, I flew to Chicago to take a workshop in design to augment my professional skills and enhance my resume. I even made an advertising contact on the plane. But my experience there confirmed my growing impression that the fees people were willing to pay for design work were often insufficient to warrant the amount of effort expended.

So in the spring of 1982, at the age of 42, I went to New York City for the first time in my life to attend a summer session at Parsons School of Design. I wanted to hone my skills so I could land a graphic design job in a larger city. I designed a letterhead on my resume that landed me my first corporate job. At this time I also painted at the Art Student League of New York. I was in heaven, but unlike heaven, knew it couldn't

Two freelance cartoons.

last. If only I could have stayed to paint for a year or two! But it was financially out of the question.

Armed with big city training, I moved to Minneapolis, found a studio apartment, and began to search for a graphic design job. It was exciting to be in a place where I could attend theatre, concerts and museums plus take classes at any of the numerous colleges in the area. Sometimes I spent an entire Saturday morning planning my agenda, with only the afternoon and Sunday to follow through. It was so cold at the bus stop that I purchased a sheepskin coat at an outlet store which was as toasty warm as taking my house with me.

Searching through the newspapers every day in the 'Help Wanted' sections, I found a five-dollar-an-hour design job at a small book publishing company. Of course, the cost of living was higher in Minneapolis; for example, while a parking meter in Stevens Point had been a dime, here it was a quarter. Every day as I passed the state

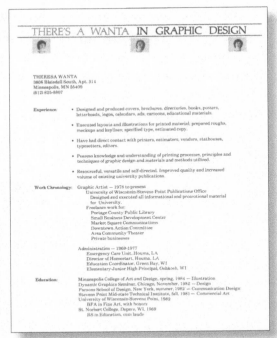

The resumé design with which I won the position of graphic designer at a major company in Minneapolis. The small images at the top of the sheet are reproduced below.

unemployment agency on my way from the bus stop to my workplace, I thought, "That's for losers."

I liked the work but had a supervisor who knew less about publishing and design than I did, and felt threatened by my ability. Again jealousy reared its ugly head. She challenged me on how I had achieved my results as a method of learning how to perform the task herself. She checked the contents of my wastebasket to be sure I wasn't wasting supplies. Even the nuns at the convent hadn't done

New York?

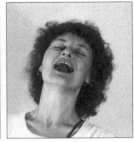

New York!

New York.

that! It didn't help when the owner told her I was the most productive employee she had ever had. I could paste up by hand an entire book in three days. Each line of copy had to be perfectly straight, all photos with accompanying captions had to be sized and cropped to fit. I was surprised that the compliment angered my supervisor.

My dear friend from Moorhead said she had never seen me so unhappy and advised me to take an unpaid day off to search for a new job. We were not allowed to use the phone at work for private purposes, and I didn't have holidays off until I had worked there a full year. In fact, to get Christmas day off, I had to put in an extra hour of work for eight days. At that time there were no cell phones and lunch was only a half hour, too short to run to the next block to use a pay phone. I decided to give two weeks' notice of my resignation. In the meantime, my supervisor quit without notice!

All of the firm's book titles had already been announced in the spring advertisements. The owner was now in a bind and asked me to stay on. By now I had taken a class in self-assertion and agreed, provided my wages were doubled from five dollars an hour to ten. Done deal. I finished the design, paste up, proofreading and production of the announced titles. In addition, I trained two replacements. Having been trained to be super conscientious, before I left, I asked the owner if there was anything else I could do. Negative.

As I walked to the bus stop, I passed the unemployment office and thought, "Why not?" I didn't expect much since I was the one who had resigned. The woman at the service window was a godsend. She had me fill out a multitude of forms and said because I had been asked to stay on, and because I had asked if there was any more work to do, I had in effect, been laid off. I therefore qualified for unemployment benefits. The publishing company objected, so I was required to attend a hearing where the owner was to be present. Here I was, barely a year in the "big city" having to confront the owner of a publishing company at a hearing. Because the owner didn't show, I automatically won the benefits. I was the first in the history of the company to do so.

I continued to do freelance work between job searches. The most prestigious assignment I received was to illustrate the cover for *The Christian Century* magazine, December, 1985. It was accepted a year after I acquired the corporate position.

Again, through the want ads, I found a graphic design position with a Fortune 500 company. My design training from the previous summer in New York had paid off. The company liked my designs and was impressed that I had studied in New York. During three interviews I was asked what had been the most negative experience in my previous job, and how I resolved it. Fortunately, because of my recent experience, these questions were easy to answer. Then in different guises, the interviewer repeatedly asked how well I got along with others, to the point where I replied, "If it's that difficult to get along with the people in this company, I'm not sure I want to work here." Bingo. Out of 100 applicants, I got the job.

The company offered an annual salary of $20,000. Again using my assertiveness training, I asked for and received an extra thousand dollars. I had all the responsibilities of an art director, sans the title. I subcontracted the services of printers, photographers, embossers, and typesetters, developed and executed concepts, and also provided customer service and did marketing. I worked with the CEO, Vice President, subsidiary managers, department heads and staff. There was more money available to develop designs, use four-color-process-printing, die cuts, and expensive papers. Paper heft often gave a printed piece extra elegance. I was allowed to develop expensive comprehensives for man-

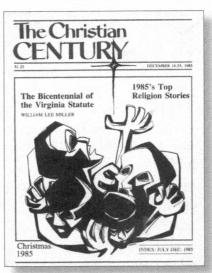

My cover illustration for *Christian Century* magazine.

agers who were unable to visualize a design from a black and white sketch. Comprehensives were one-of-a-kind close approximates of what the printed piece would look like. This was before computers could easily produce a composite.

Management sometimes asked for three different designs and had a committee evaluate them. Then they asked, "Can't you put a little of each design into one?!" It seems everyone wanted to have their finger in the pie so they could claim credit for the design. I learned the fastest way to gain approval of a design was to leave a glaring error. The justifiable corrective input left the design itself intact. In my art classes I had learned that Rembrandt, after painting a portrait and letting it dry, would sometimes deliberately paint a distorted nose over the dried one. As expected, the patron immediately criticized it. Then Rembrandt took it to his studio, wiped off the distortion, waited a respectable amount of time, and presented it to the client again, who was now pleased with the results.

All in all, this was a good job, and I was doing what I liked. In fact there were times when I enjoyed the challenge of convincing management to accept a design. If they did not appreciate the value of using white space in a brochure, I went into an explanation of how empty or "white" space gave the eye a place to rest, and how this space contrasted with the printed words to emphasize them. Some accepted my professional advice, others said, "I'm paying for the paper, so I want every bit of it filled with copy."

Department managers sent letters complimenting me on my work. At first, I thought it rather silly; after all, this was my job and I was getting paid to do it. But after all these years, when I look in my files, there they are! There is more than one from the CEO of the company himself, several from Corporate Relations and other departments as well as from the Minneapolis Chamber Symphony.

When asked to design the collateral for the United Way Campaign for the company, the Vice-President of Corporate Relations would not accept my initial concept. I developed several other ideas which continued to be rejected though the deadline was drawing near. He then approved the initial concept with only two weeks' time to execute it. Photographers, writers, typesetters, paper suppliers and printers rushed to get their part of the project done by deadline. It won first place statewide. When the award was given at a luncheon, the Vice-President went up to accept the trophy without acknowledging the rest of us who had worked hard to execute the concept on time.

On my way to work each morning, I brought my briefcase on the bus, appearing quite the professional. Little did anyone know that sometimes it held my ice skates. Whenever I could manage it during lunch time, I took the bus from the office just a few blocks

One of the awards we won for a project.

away to Peavey Plaza. Once the corporate photographer took my photo and had it published in the company newsletter.

At one point I was asked to participate in the corporate fashion show with nine other women. What fun!

While employed by this company, I purchased decent furniture and saved enough to buy my first brand new car; a red Toyota Tercel hatchback. I had done a great deal of research before the purchase. As I tried to compare prices among the dealers, I met one who told me to sign on the dotted line; that it didn't mean I had to buy the car. I pointed out the fine print beneath the line which stated that a signature was a contract to purchase and refused to sign.

At another dealer, the salesman refused to give a price, objecting that I would only use it for comparative shopping. Duh! I walked out of the display room. He came running out after me in the parking lot. After a few more dealership visits that day, I made the purchase and paid almost all in cash. The next day, the man who had chased me to the parking lot called me at work to say he had a good deal for me. He was quite surprised when I told him, "Too late, I've already made a purchase." The next weekend, I drove 200 miles to show my first brand new car to my parents. My father's assessment was, "That's not a good car."

My friends in Stevens Point had kept in touch, and they invited me to join them to cross country ski at Ely, Minnesota, where one of them had free access to a cottage. After skiing a full day, we gathered in the car and passed around a bottle of Amaretto before heading back to the cottage. My friends in Moorhead often invited me to visit. One summer I was included in a fishing party near Detroit Lakes. It was nice that the men didn't mind

Ice skating at Peavey Plaza in downtown Minneapolis during lunch break.

baiting the hooks. We went out on a boat which included one of the anglers' blind father. He caught a fish by feeling the tautness of the line! I was lucky, too. We were the only two who caught fish that day.

During the fourth year at this company, I developed severe repetitive strain injuries to both hands. It could hardly have been otherwise. I had been working by hand with T-squares, triangles, exacto knives, hot wax and hand burnishers. I designed, did layouts and pasted up the annual and SEC reports, brochures, magazines, newsletters and the like. Like a good girl, I never missed a deadline, and was proud of it.

Sometimes the copy was changed at the last minute and I had to have it re-typeset and then mortise it in, in perfect alignment with the rest of the sentence or paragraph. When planning a large project such as the company annual report, we included all the players in the scheduling and planning process. I always built in two extra weeks of cushion time to allow for unexpected delays. Inevitably, at the last minute, parts were rewritten which then had to pass through a lengthy approval process before being typeset and re-pasted. Once because of these copy changes, the project was completed too late for

Cross-country skiing in Ely, Minnesota, with friends.

in-house printing and had to be contracted to an outside printer as a rush job at twice the normal cost. Usually management objected to paying an outside printer. But since they were the ones who had held up the process, they had no good reason to grouse.

It was all extremely stressful. Anyone who has worked in print publishing knows how many variables are at risk. Sometimes the in-house printer dropped in all the photos upside down in a brochure, thus jeopardizing the deadline. If I tried to do something different, the printers protested, "It can't be done!" When I showed samples of having done it at the university, a nonprofit, they did it and did it well.

When I first mentioned the increasing pain in my hands, no one believed me because there was no evidence of carpal tunnel syndrome. I began to doubt my own sanity. If I used my hands, the fingers would

Beginner's luck fishing with my friends from Moorhead.

swell. By the time I obtained a doctor appointment, the swelling was down. I developed anxiety and worried how I would support myself without the use my hands. The pain was exacerbated when I tried to comb my hair, open my mail, or turn a doorknob. I could barely write and had to hire someone to address my Christmas cards. I could not apply enough pressure for my signature to appear on the carbon copy of a credit card purchase.

Driving was a pain, but opening the car door was worse. I began to have panic attacks. In the past, I had heard of such things, but in my hubris, I considered them imaginary ailments. The pain I experienced was cumulative, forcing me to stagger the use of my hands. My friends from Moorhead traveled 250 miles to pick me up and care for me for a week. Their daughter buttered my bread, which was something I could not do for myself.

Finally, my condition was correctly diagnosed as repetitive strain injury, or tendinitis, in both hands.

I implemented ice therapies and hand exercises and wore wrist braces. The physical therapist taught me small tricks to get around the most painful tasks such as carrying groceries, placing a pot of water on the stove and wringing out a cloth. I could not slice bread, nor fill the gas tank of my car. I was awarded worker's compensation for a year. The attorney offered to have his friend invest the amount for

Two of my corporate graphic designs.

me. I asked what I would live on in the meantime. Although I could not tie my shoes, I once went roller skating around Lake of the Isles, asking perfect strangers to lace up my skates. It felt good to be able to perform this activity and gave me a sense of power.

The year 1988 was full of challenges: I had major surgery, my apartment was burglarized, and I lost my job. When I all but lost the use of my hands, I thought the condition would last forever. I mourned not having traveled more or having pursued a master's degree in fine art. But slowly my hands began to heal, and one morning, about a year after the onset of the affliction, I woke up to find the pain had left me. As strange as it may sound, I missed this constant companion. It felt as though a reliable friend had gone. I still had to be careful not to keyboard for more than an hour at a time and only a few times a week to prevent triggering pain for days. I still had to be careful not to push, pull, or carry heavier objects. Doors were difficult. On the bus, I steadied myself by the crook of my elbow around the pole and carried things in a bag over my shoulder. I carried a teeny, tiny purse. But I had gotten better.

I took any job I could get, all at minimum wage. Good thing I was still glib of tongue, for I began conducting workshops on art at a venue in Minneapolis called Open University and at Artsign, a Minneapolis art supply store. Then I devised a series of my own art classes called, "Want-a-Workshop" which I held at the Midway Motor Lodge. I was surprised to receive requests for scholarships from prospective students. I learned that if I took the initiative, people attributed power to me. Supply companies sent me catalogs. It was sporadic income, so I kept looking for ways to supplement it.

When I was finally able to press the buttons on the phone, I took on a job in the dreaded field of telemarketing. In my first interview, the manager pointed to the piranha-filled aquarium in her office and said, "This is what I want you to be." I walked out. The next telemarketing job was in carpet cleaning, no less. The job was listed at five dollars an hour, but when we got there, we were paid a dollar less. Normally, I would have challenged this, but I was beginning to lose my fighting spirit. I learned to overcome the fear of cold calling, a skill that served me in good stead later when I began marketing my art. Surprisingly, I became one of two top sellers. It was a numbers game; the more calls I made, the more orders I received. Voicemail messages were unbelievable: babies and dogs played their parts to leave entertaining messages. Some families sang in chorus. Many Hmong families were on the call list though they could not speak English at that time. I learned that each family had a designated English speaking member.

When we obtained an order, the manager pretended to calculate a customized price to the customer, but it was the same for everyone. From these prospective clients I learned the kindest way to reject a telemarketing call is to say, "I am not interested." No need to invent a family funeral. When I found a better job, I quit. The manager called me the following week, offering to pay me the full five dollars an hour. I declined this 20 percent pay increase since I had found a better paying part-time reception-ist job at a hospital in downtown Saint Paul. It was mostly verbal in nature, interacting with and receiv-ing patients. Perfect. Then I was

When I left the corporation, I received this farewell card from my department illustrated by Bob from the Printing Department. I often wore a sailor's uniform I got from the Navy surplus store.

asked to do some typing. I was good at it and so received more. And more. My hands began to swell so I had to leave. I met a nurse there who remains a friend to this day. The pattern of receiving typing as-signments for jobs described as verbal in nature persisted, thus limit-ing my options.

Once I was interviewed, at five dollars an hour of course, for a customer service job. I was to take calls from customers who had questions regarding their purchase of kits of educational materials. Since I had a background in education and customer service, I presented my overqualified resume to the interviewer who appeared to be in his twenties. "Hmmm. Looks like you don't have much phone experience," he said.

When I applied for professional jobs commensurate with my experience, yet another degree was required and I already had three of them. Often the interviewers who themselves had learned on the job now had high standards for a new hire. I applied unsuccessfully for metropolitan, state, and federal jobs. These required taking tests and filling out mountains of application forms. Employment agencies touted the value of "transferable skills," and I emphasized mine during interviews. More often than not, I was told, "but you haven't done it at *this* company." I never understood how managers and CEOs migrated from one company to another without skipping a beat. Going back to teaching elementary school required specialty degrees even in teaching reading to young children. I don't know how every one of my first graders, some without kindergarten, had learned to read twenty-five years ago when I had taught them with only two years of college.

The job hunt was interesting. I had so little to lose; I could experiment with various approaches. I had to find something that did not require extensive use of my hands. In those days, the forms always had a question asking if the applicant had a disability. That was disabling in itself. The way I got the job at the greenhouse was by responding to a want ad two weeks after it had been published. In my cover letter I wrote: "By now you must have a high stack of resumes. Why not save time and just hire me?" I got the job. Though it paid only five dollars an hour, at least it was more pleasant. Creative, it was not. We had to arrange the bouquets exactly as they appeared on the advertising photos, and do so quickly. One of the employees kept giving me directives, causing me to wonder what was going on. No one had introduced her to me as my supervisor.

At the same time I worked as a national account executive in graphic slide sales, as opposed to today's discs. Base pay: the ubiquitous five dollars per hour. Again it was a numbers game. The hard part was, the production staff was reluctant to fulfill the orders, so we were caught between the customer and the production staff. There was something odd about this company. I wondered if it was a tax write-off. One Friday they didn't pay us, so the next Monday I didn't show up. The manager called. With the voice of experience I said I didn't work for free. From then on, I was the only one in the company who got paid until I found a more reliable job. Later I learned that the company had folded.

As a Security and Information Officer I worked at a conservatory and sculpture garden in Minneapolis, a rather prestigious job with the nonprestigious wage of five dollars per hour. I carried with me a two-way radio. I enjoyed interacting with visitors and expounding on Frank Gehry's glass fish sculpture, but it was another dead-end job which I supplemented with temporary employment.

Contracting with two temporary employment agencies, I enjoyed working for a variety of companies. Many of the assignments required driving out to unfamiliar suburban addresses during morning rush hour. Obsessed with being on time, I left home extra early. Many well-meaning friends suggested it might be possible to work myself into a full-time position. Nada. Nyet. Nope. There was a caveat in the contract to nix that. Even combined, these temp jobs didn't provide enough income. I had to refuse many offers because most of them required extensive keyboarding. Once I thought, "How bad can my hands really be after all these years?" Maybe it was all a figment of my imagination. Wrong. I accepted a keyboarding position and suffered the consequences.

I did, however get a fairly lengthy stint with a beer wholesaler association in downtown Saint Paul for $12 an hour. The director was a woman who was one of the best and most intelligent of bosses I've had. It was a great job requiring mostly verbal skills until the director retired and the office reorganized and relocated. I continued a friendship with the director.

Then a good paying job came my way in a Minnetonka real estate office, clear across the other side of Saint Paul and Minneapolis. I always left home early, about two hours early, to miss the bulk of the traffic on the freeways. Once it was snowing heavily. A pick-up truck speedily entered the freeway on my right, skidded across in front of me and struck the guard rail on my left. Whew! On my way home that evening, a red car passed me on the right, executed a 360 degree spinout directly in front of me in my lane, ended up facing forward and kept going. Whew, whew! I know that it was pure luck that I was alive that day. The promised job description did not materialize, so the job responsibilities grew, the lunch hour shrank, and I was paged during my break. I couldn't keep pace and reluctantly left.

One of my part-time jobs was working at a library, this time in Saint Paul. I was the new kid on the block and couldn't understand why the latest new hire expressed such great relief. I soon found out. There was an African American employee who always harassed the newest hire, sensing that a Caucasian would be afraid to speak up lest it be construed as prejudice. After a time, I reported the problem to the supervisor who advised me to attempt to settle it privately. I did. The vocabulary unleashed by the employee turned the air blue.

I reported to the Supervisor again. She decided the three of us would meet. When we did, the offending employee swiveled her chair with her back toward us. The supervisor whispered something in her ear, and the meeting was over. The union called me and asked if I wanted to pursue reverse discrimination. I decided not to, since the point had been made and the harassment cycle broken. I considered leaving because I knew it would be uncomfortable working alongside the offending employee and also feared retaliation. In the end, the deciding factor was that my hands were beginning to rebel against handling so many books even on a half-day basis.

Simultaneously, I worked as a part time student recruiter at a for-profit school of communication. It was the strangest of my jobs. Since the phones were kept locked, every day I had to request mine be unlocked, in order to set up appointments with nonprofit job placement organizations. These job counseling agencies offered government subsidized training for their clientele to make them employable. It was my job to convince the staff to choose our communications school for training. As I traveled to these nonprofit agencies I had to account for my time by keeping records on three different forms, of mileage, destinations, names of organizations, individuals visited and results obtained. Each form required essentially the same information but in different configurations. I also was to record the time I left, arrived and returned for each visit which in itself took many minutes.

The desk I used was also locked so I had to get supplies from the main desk in the hallway where all the supplies were inventoried and listed on sheets of paper mounted on the wall corresponding to the desk drawers. When I started this job, many promises had been made, none of which were kept. I wrote an audacious letter stating "that it had come to my attention" etc. The next day I was called into the office, given a larger than usual check and was bid "goodbye." I think I was fired. I wasn't sure because I had never experienced it before. This was not the last I would hear of this school.

Next, I applied for a nonprofit job counseling service for difficult-to-hire people. I filled out the application form without trying very hard, and even stated that I had run my own design business for a while. It seemed that employers usually found that threatening, so I was sure I wouldn't get this job. By this time I had collected more than 125 rejection letters—quite a stack. This, in the days when employers had the courtesy to send them. But I did get the job! And it was because I *had* run my own freelance business. It was the only application I hadn't bothered to copy because I was so sure I wouldn't get an interview. The job was to counsel and authorize state and federal funding for training people who were older, getting off welfare, or had personality problems.

A co-worker at this nonprofit job said, "I know you! You once came in representing the for-profit communications school. I have your card in my drawer." And so she had. We were warned not to authorize state and federal funding for training at that school because it charged exorbitant prices for tuition and made employment placement promises it didn't keep. Later we heard a news report that the FBI had closed it down for fraud. We laughed about it, and everyone teased me.

I liked this job. It paid a decent salary; my coworkers were fun and the work was rewarding. I met with new clients almost every day.

We did not yet have computers, but kept handwritten records on each client. The manager was hard working, efficient and conscientious. No mismanagement of state or federal funds here. Our job placement numbers were high partially due to good screening practices. That was just as well. Why use public money for those who would not cooperate or had no potential? Because of our placement success rate, we qualified for many grants.

In the back of my mind, I still wanted to acquire a Master's degree in Fine Art at a figurative art school in New York, so I carefully saved my income. My hands were pretty good now, and at my age, I wanted to do this before something else would break, a premonition wisely heeded, as it turned out. My ultimate goal was to teach figure drawing and painting at the university level for which the degree was a requirement. It would be a perfect job because I could use my voice more than my hands in a field I liked. My research and personal interviews showed there was a good job outlook for this career. There was a projected shortage of instructors in this liberal arts field because computers were beginning to dominate the employment field. After a time, I discussed my plans with my manager and she agreed to release me from my contract.

4

Oh, the Places I've Lived

In my lifetime I have moved more than thirty-seven times. Ten of the moves took place while I was in the convent, excluding summer school and summer assignments. Many people my age wonder why I moved so often, not realizing I started later in life with no secular job history, contacts, or savings, not to mention secular savvy. As a result, I had to seek out the least costly rentals. Others of my age had purchased houses at 1962 prices in quiet suburban locations.

Finding an inexpensive place to live accounted for thin walls resulting in being subjected to unwanted noise. Being older, my noise tolerance level was not that of a twenty-year-old. I found it surprising that some tenants did not sleep at night. Not experienced in renters' rights, I was even more surprised that some landlords did not keep their word. One never knows what a building is like until one lives in it, and then is stuck with the situation for a year, when the lease is up for renewal. Then I had to scramble, balancing the notice date of the old apartment with the availability date of a new apartment. This sometimes resulted in settling for another unsatisfactory place.

I made several moves to continue my education out of state, and sometimes the building I lived in was sold or remodeled. Occasionally I moved to be nearer my work site. Once I moved because my apartment was burgled.

But I did get to know neighborhoods I would never have chosen had I better financial means. I got to share a building with various ethnic groups which I found enriching. While most of the places I lived were pleasant as is to be expected, I thought it might be an eye opener as well as entertaining to describe the exceptions. Even so, I have tried to include positive aspects of these less desirable places.

A dear friend, acknowledging my latest move, wrote a limerick to the effect of:

There once was a woman named Terry,
Who in life was known not to tarry,
She's found a new home,
Ne'er more to roam (she says)
Each move leaving less to carry.

And that was true. I didn't accumulate much because of the frequent moves: I got rid of things before each move, and afterward purged more, wondering why I had bothered to pack it to begin with. It came to a point where I saved the packing boxes in anticipation of a possible next move. I devised a checklist of necessary notifications for each move. About one third of my possessions were paintings, art equipment, and art supplies. I never became overly attached to a place. Perhaps I had been conditioned by my early convent years when we were transferred at the will of the Mother Superior. Whenever I met friends, they did not ask what I had been doing, but rather, "Where do you live now?" I think an appropriate epitaph for me will be, "She finally stopped moving!"

In 1987, when I was living in an apartment in Stevens Square in Minneapolis, the caretaker lived directly above me, playing the bass on his stereo as loud as could be. It did not please him when I asked him to turn it down. In the meantime, I had major surgery. On returning from the hospital, I found the plaster of the ceiling had collapsed right below where his stereo was standing!

A few days later, lying in bed on a sultry Sunday morning, still recuperating with sixteen stitches across my abdomen, I heard strange noises. It sounded as though someone outside was raiding the trash bin for soda cans. It was about 5:30 a.m. Since I'm an early riser, I was about to get up to satisfy my curiosity when I remembered the doctor's order to get as much rest as possible. Twenty minutes later, I heard floorboards creaking in my bedroom. I could barely see without my glasses, but made out the form of a dark, slight built young man.

Rather than responding with fear, I was outraged at this invasion of my privacy and shouted, "WHO LET YOU IN HERE?" emphatically accenting each word. I reached for something to throw, though there wasn't much on the shelf next to me. I guessed that he thought I was reaching for a weapon, because he made a hurried exit, feet pounding down the hallway. I waited until I could no longer hear him. I was in no condition to confront an intruder. Doors peeped open in the hallway.

Now I could see what had caused the strange noise: the intruder had cut through the screen and crawled in through the narrow French window in the living room of my first floor apartment. Since there was a high basement, he must have hoisted himself up on the manager's car parked next to the building. He had been in my apartment for those twenty minutes helping himself to my laundry quarters, my little red purse, and the ten-dollar bill lying next to it. I dressed as hurriedly as possible, circled the building and checked the alley and adjacent streets, peeking into trash bins searching for my little red purse.

I called the police. The next day a detective arrived to take fingerprints with his kit of tape, white and black dusting powders and ostrich feather brush. There were only useless partial or smudged prints taken from the window frame and the round, decorative china box which had held the quarters. I was grateful the beautiful box had not been taken because it had been a gift from a co-worker at the children's home in Louisiana.

Later, my credit cards and company ID were reported as having been found along the railroad tracks about a mile from my work place. Coincidentally, the cards were found by a paper supply company with whom I had conducted business at the corporation. When I returned to work, there they were on my desk, though I had long since canceled the credit cards.

I missed most the small, sleek coin purse tucked inside the other purse. I had purchased it at Saks Fifth Avenue in New York two years earlier. It was deep red polished leather and always looked flat, no matter how many coins it held. I remember thinking at the time I bought it that I should really buy two. Never have I wished so much that I had! In my subsequent trips to New York, I always stopped in at Saks to see if perhaps they had another like it, but never found one.

The building owner, not to be confused with the caretaker, allowed me to wallpaper the bedroom, and in fact, paid for the wallpaper. The old wallpaper had two worn, gray spots just above the headboard where years of heads had leaned against the wall. I had never wallpapered before, but had seen it done at home. Besides I could read. My theory was if I could read the instructions, I should be able to do it. It turned out perfectly. I invited the owner to take a look at it, but he never did, trusting that I had done an adequate job.

When I smelled gas in the building, I knocked on the caretaker's door. He answered the door in his speedos and was visibly irritated to be disturbed. Was I expecting a "Thank you", perhaps? This caretaker did not follow the law that required giving the tenant notice before entering their apartment. One winter day, I left to do a few errands and returned to find a slightly familiar looking pair of Ray-ban sunglasses on my table along with the warmest pair of men's winter gloves I was ever to wear.

It was at this time that I had an experience that was stranger than fiction. I decided to take evening art classes at an atelier at Calhoun Square in Minneapolis. Class started at 7:30 p.m. and I was late. I parked on Lagoon avenue where it curved into Hennepin Avenue and quickly left my car, clasping my unwieldy drawing materials. I realized I didn't have my purse but knew I had locked my car as I felt my pocketed key.

It was about 10 p.m. when I returned from class and when I looked for my little red purse in the car, it wasn't there. I looked under the car, no purse. Had I left it at home? In vain I went back to check my apartment, then the car again, and once more my apartment. And then I knew. It must have fallen off my lap when in such haste I had hopped out of the car to attend class. What chance was there that I would find it?

My intuition drove me back to Lagoon Avenue and I parked my car in the very same spot as before. No purse there, of course. I thought I might find some of its contents if I walked up the block toward Hennepin and back down the other side of the street, my eyes searching to the left and right not unlike a blind person's cane. As I walked down the street across from my car, two scruffy looking men came toward me, each carrying a small plastic bag. They looked a little spooky, but to my relief, crossed the street to where my car was. I walked to the end of the block and then cautiously over to the same side of the street they were on. The two men stood by my car, staring at it in disbelief.

A bit afraid, I went up to my car door and inserted the key, The men looked at me and the younger one asked, "Did you lose this purse?" I recognized it immediately as he pulled it out of his plastic bag.

I excitedly told them I could hardly believe it was the purse I had been looking for. They said they had found it earlier in the evening beside my car.

The older of the two told me to state my name to make sure I was the true owner. (!) The younger then gave me the purse, but the money was gone. Tempting fate, I said, "I had money in it." He replied, "Yes about $50, as he pulled the money out of his pocket. I rewarded each with a ten dollar bill, but the older man refused his, saying, "No, *he* found it," pointing to the younger, and handed his ten back to me. At this point, the younger was trying to give me back the five dollars' worth of loose change from the purse, again in a plastic bag. I told him to keep it. He tried to return his ten dollar bill as if in trade, but I insisted he keep that, too.

Then these two talked about how it must have been the spirit that caused us to be there at the same time, now about 11 p.m. Strangely unafraid, but still cautious, I agreed. We talked a little as the moon made its appearance above us. Then I left, not wanting to press my luck. The whole experience was so strange, that I immediately wrote it down when I got home, my little red purse lying beside me on the table. I knew if I did not document it, I would not believe it myself.

Update: About twenty years later, when a friend from Minneapolis read this story, she said she thought the two men might have been Native Americans, based on the research she had done when writing her book, *The Life of Emily Peak: One Dedicated Ojibwe*. It had been her observation that they are outreaching in their own way, look out for the other and share what they have--even among the street people in downtown Minneapolis.

In 1989 I moved to The Commodore in Saint Paul. This was the most elegant, well situated apartment I've lived in. Most of the units were condominiums in a historic building. In fact, Scott Fitzgerald had lived there at one time. The odd thing was, the heating coils were in the ceiling. Fine if you lived on any floor but the first, and I lived on the first. While a radiatior had been installed to supply supplemental heating, its use was very expensive. The unit had its own washer and dryer. Such luxury! I made friends with a woman who lived on Summit Avenue and had a summer art studio in the basement of the building. I regretted leaving this place but wanted to pursue studies in New York to obtain a Master of Fine Arts degree. After graduation, another friend in that building graciously let me stay with her until I found another apartment.

After returning from New York, I lived in a very small one-bedroom apartment situated in a beautiful Victorian neighborhood. It was so tiny I deliberated whether I should, in fact, agree to take it. The landlord promised, "Oh, all this furniture will be out of here," as if I would not have furniture of my own! I worked part time while the landlord graciously let me hold studio shows for the neighborhood. She even commissioned me to do a house portrait. I did not want my New York training to go to waste. I moved all the furniture out of the apartment into the back hall. But would anyone attend? Attend they did, and they purchased my work. So began a 12 year period of selling my paintings. After four years, the landlord began to renovate the building, forcing me to move on.

(above) On the far left, I celebrate my 50th birthday at the Commodore courtyard with family.

(below) Here, second from right, I celebrate again with my dearest friends from Moorhead and Germany.

A friend from London (standing) came to visit me in my studio.

Still in Saint Paul, I had trouble finding an apartment since now in 1998 the availability rate for rentals was at one and one half percent. The only place I could find was located in Frogtown, away from my former lovely neighborhood. In the mornings even at 5:30 a.m., I saw drug dealers on the corner. Acting the part of a little old lady, I politely greeted them with a "Good Morning" and kept walking. They always responded equally politely. I knew that as long as I did not indicate recognition of what they were doing, I would be safe. Now I understood why people did not report drug dealers in inner cities. When I held studio shows, my loyal patrons came from Summit Avenue and noted the drug deals going on in broad daylight. They were unruffled because their now beautiful homes had been rescued from such goings on years before.

For exercise, I walked every morning and evening in this rather economically depressed area. Mothers who sat on their front porches in the evening would not let their small children talk to me during my evening walk. I was puzzled, since as a former school teacher, I was accustomed to engaging children in conversation if their parents were present. Then it dawned on me. They thought I was a streetwalker!

Eventually when I started conversations with the mothers, they began to trust me. When I met a little girl on her bike, she stopped and said, "Guess what my name is." I took a chance, drawing upon my many associations with various ethnic children and guessed, "Samantha." That little girl was duly impressed: "How did you know?" I equally impressed myself.

Once a small, stoned or drunken man wobbled closely behind me as I quickly darted into the house. Just before I did, he asked, "Can I come in your house?" The woman across the street would not let anyone park near her house because she was saving the space for her son when he returned from work. It wasn't worth pursuing the issue. While we had no block parties, what formed community was having a window smashed in each of our cars on the same rainy night. It got everyone talking with one another the next morning.

When I returned from the farmers' market one Saturday morning, I noticed a car on my side of the street with its lights left on. With a bouquet of red and pink peonies still in my arms, I knocked on the door of my rather seedy looking neighbor. Not sure what to expect I said "Excuse me," to which he replied, "Why, did you sneeze?" The car was his and I knew then that I had made an ally forever.

At the time I had moved into the second story of that apartment, I noticed a freshly plastered ceiling in the alcove off the living room. Good, I thought, this landlord takes care of his property. Nevertheless, I was puzzled that the can of plaster and the stepladder had been left there. After the next rainfall, I understood.

Then there was the time the FBI came to my door, flashing their IDs just like in the movies. A man and a woman. "Nice paintings," the woman said as they looked around. They asked my name, how long I had lived there, and who had lived there before me. Since I didn't know, I gave them the contact information for my landlord. I suspected there had been drug activity.

I had been hearing a scratching sound in the wall of the studio for some time but did not see anything on the surface. I reported it to the landlord who insisted no creature could get in since there was no soffit there.

One afternoon as I was painting, I sensed I was being watched. I turned around and there was a beady-eyed squirrel standing upright staring at me. I chased it hither and yon as it knocked off my jars of paint brushes from the window sill, urinated on the watercolor papers on my drafting table and then had the audacity to refresh itself with a drink of water from the tray on the radiator. It scampered across my palette of paint, picking up blue pigment which it promptly stenciled upon my upholstered folding chair. When its paws keyboarded across my laptop, it brought up messages I had never seen before. I knew things were getting dangerous when the varmint began to chatter.

Finally, I figured out that the thing to do was to pull all the blinds to block out the light, confine the rodent to the room that led to the stairwell, put on the light there to attract it, and open the door to the basement. I couldn't open the door to the outside for fear someone might walk in off the street. As soon as the little beast left, I slammed shut the basement door. After a short while, I opened the door, and there he was; Mr. Beady Eyes, ready to pounce. Slam. Then the tenant downstairs opened the cellar door that led to the back yard, and that was the end of that. I had not thought to look behind a painting propped up against the wall which disclosed a hole gnawed out through the sheetrock. Later I noticed that squirrels darted in and out of the attic through the eaves with ease.

After a year in Frogtown, I found a place back in my old neighborhood, this time on Dayton Avenue. Would I be allowed to paint if I contracted this apartment? The caretaker assured me I could. I repeated the question to be sure, and he responded in the affirmative again. Foolishly, I did not get it in writing. I was pleased he allowed me to hold art shows in my unit and to install moldings from which to suspend my paintings.

What I liked about this place was that it had a lovely three season back porch with tree branches draping over it. It was like living in a tree house. The caretaker permitted me to design a flower garden in the back yard which was satisfying to me and enjoyed by all the tenants. I had slowly dug it up, a few shovelfuls a day since I was still favoring my back, and had topsoil brought in by the Boy Scouts. After three years it had matured into a lovely display.

Of course, after the work had been done, a new tenant wanted to have a garden within this garden. Since I did not own the property, I agreed to compromise. Then her dog used it for a toilet. When this tenant initially moved into the unit below me, I asked her to tell me if she ever smelled an odor from my painting. But no! She went straight to the caretaker and complained. He took her side, and I had to leave. A year later, I learned she moved out anyway. Lesson learned: get it in writing.

Another problem with most of the apartments I lived in was that I could hear the noise from adjacent apartments. In this apartment it was especially disconcerting because the caretaker had his enthusiastic girlfriend over on a regular basis. I wondered why he got a discount on his rent when he didn't know how to remove the handle of a faucet. I had to show him how to pop off the top to reveal the screw.

So now, still in the beautiful neighborhood, I moved to Virginia Street. Three dogs in the building had been barking since December when I moved in, one of them a beagle that howled at 2:00 a.m. After doing a one-on-one request with two of the offending dog owners, I was at my wit's end.

The third dog was owned by a long-term tenant who tethered the animal right at the front door where it barked every day from 3 to 5 p.m. It was impossible to enter the building without stepping over it, no small feat in winter while struggling to unlock the door with arms overflowing with groceries. I feared dropping the groceries on its dear head. The dog relieved itself for the rest of winter as the yellow snow around the entrance gave way to burned out grass in spring.

One May morning as I rushed off to work, the next-door neighbor woman lurched out of nowhere and accosted me: "This is a dog neighborhood and I am here to speak on behalf of a tenant in your building because we think you have complained about her dog."

I used my swearing-in hand gesture as I stated eyeball-to-eyeball that I had not complained about any dogs barking since December. She then hailed the tenant from my building who said, "I found a note on my door from the building owner and it said that he was not going to lose a good paying tenant over my dog!" I always paid my rent a week in advance, thus currying favor with the landlord. I reiterated my oath regarding the sole action I had taken in December. I said that I had to leave for work and got into my car.

As the engine turned over, so did a realization in my mind. Suddenly I remembered that although I had not complained about the tenant's dog barking, I had about her dog's incontinence. It had completely slipped my mind, lending eye-contact honesty to my lie.

In 2005 I bought a new condo in downtown Saint Paul. The builder promised that extra measures had been taken to ensure that noise would be at a minimum in the building. But wonder of wonders: there were sliding doors in the units which rattled across the doorways ending in a "boom"! Some tenants immediately did it quietly when made aware of it, while others would not be "told what to do." Such was the case of the woman who lived above me. The trash chute went right through my bedroom wall. The builder assured me that the metal ties connecting the metal chute to the wooden studs would deaden the sound, hence equating a "party wall." I saw it as a case of "redefine and conquer." Tenants threw their trash down at ungodly hours. Management refused to install a lock for those hours.

This unit was across from a hotel where tour buses loudly idled their engines all day. When I talked to one bus driver, he said, "Lady, you have to understand these people leave their lunches on the bus so we have to keep it running to keep these lunches air conditioned." To which I replied, "You have to understand that we live here and have to listen to that noise all day." Discussions with hotel management were sometimes successful and sometimes not, depending on whom I talked to. The best solution was to leave my unit for the day.

Also across from my unit stood an energy company which produced constant noise. Though the company was compliant with city standards for decibel levels, the levels were set by officials who lived far away from those decibels. I could never sit out on the deck to quietly read a book or watch the sunrise.

Finally, immediately after we signed our contract, the management company raised the association fee. Since this was the first time I had purchased a condo, I thought I had not researched the company thoroughly enough. But after conferring with other owners among whom were lawyers, property managers and business owners, I learned the wool had been pulled over their eyes, too. After three years, only two out of the original 42 tenants remained.

On a positive note, I made friends with Ethiopian, Vietnamese and Somali families. We invited each other over for meals and I got to know their children. The Vietnamese mother, who had a prodigy four-year-old and a new baby, showed me her wedding pictures from her original country, made the best spring rolls I have ever tasted, and told of her father being left behind in that well-publicized last flight out of Vietnam. From the Ethiopian mother I learned to prepare Ethiopian food. After helping her oldest son interpret their financial statements, she gave me a beautiful ethnic dress woven on a hand loom in her country which I still cherish. Sometimes I had a dinner party for these new friends to meet my old friends. I also got to know a Caucasian couple with whom I have maintained a friendship to this day.

I decided to move back to small Stevens Point, Wisconsin, where I had worked before moving to Minneapolis, where surely it would be quiet. Not necessarily so. The boys across the street revved their car engines all day on Saturdays and Sundays, I guessed they perforated the mufflers. They blasted their car radios whenever they drove in and out. In the middle of the night, trains blew their whistles twice for each of the thirteen crossings. I moved to another place only to find the trains shifted cars at night, coupling them with loud "booms" which reiterated throughout the length of the train.

The landlord was congenial, allowing me to plant a garden on the property. He even tilled it. I conscientiously weeded the Chinese elm which had roots up to five feet long. He let me use water and a hose from his property. I enjoyed watching the Baltimore orioles sip the morning dew collected in the vortex of the Swiss chard, and to see bumblebees slumbering in the throats of the morning glories. Everything was hunky-dory.

What I had especially liked about this place was the deck off the living room that looked out over an orchard. By the end of summer, two trees hung low with ripe cherries. One day a flock of brown thrashers flew in and picked off about half the cherries. The next day, they flew in and polished off the rest of them. Just like that.

There were garages for each tenant, side by side, each with their own driveway. The tenant next to mine parked her vehicle behind my car, blocking it in my own driveway because her boyfriend parked his car in her driveway. Unbelievably, she left nasty notes on my car window telling me move my car! I tried to negotiate without success. The landlord would not return my calls. I finally resolved it by calling the police. That was the end of the hunky-dory. Without discussion, the hose disappeared and the garden was locked, and that after I had just finished spring planting.

After I had reported at two-week intervals that the dishwasher would not function, the landlord said, "I'm tired of hearing you complain." I responded with, "And I'm tired of complaining about it." He repaired it promptly.

During this time I enjoyed taking Learning Is ForEver classes offered by the University of Wisconsin–Stevens Point. One of the programs offered an explanation of aerodynamics as well as a free flight in a private plane. I flew in a shiny aluminum 1947 Ercoupe single engine plane. The pilot and owner, Syd, took his hands off the wheel and allowed me to bank right and left (all ever so gently) and to point the nose up and then down. We stayed up there for twenty minutes while we circled the city at 1,000 feet at 100 mph with the canopy open. Now I could say, "I flew the Coupe." The pilot memorialized the flight by giving me a signed certificate confirming it. This kept me 'flying high' for a while.

Next, I moved into another apartment operated by a newly divorced landlord. She cleaned the rooms but forgot about the dirt and cat food on the bathroom floor, as well as the cat urine on top of the refrigerator and in the cupboard. I let it go and cleaned them myself, thinking that she might be going through a difficult time in her life. When I moved out, she ignored my requests to inspect the

Flying high in a 1947 Ercoupe.

apartment but afterward withheld some of my rental deposit because she considered the floor of one room "somewhat dusty." The movers said they had never seen such a clean apartment upon the departure of a tenant. During thirty-five years of renting, I had never had my deposit money withheld. After arguing the point, I was remunerated.

Although it had been enjoyable reconnecting with old friends and making new ones, I decided to return to St. Paul, since now I missed the mixed ethnic population and the many cultural opportunities.

Things were beginning to change in the rental world. Management was not as honest or reliable as in the past. I have observed that many tenants are destructive and have less than stellar housekeeping habits which may account for the change. Some depart in the middle of the night, leaving their apartments in a mess. I was soon to learn, however, that now managers were beginning to make errors in recording my rental payments.

The rental market had tightened considerably when I returned to St. Paul in 2014. I had to settle for something on Como Avenue *near the railroad tracks!* Management promised that the train ran only during daytime on the track fifteen feet from my bedroom. It turned out that seventy-four trains ran twenty-four hours a day. Despite my ear plugs, the diesel engines and over a hundred oil tankers shattered my sleep several times every single night. I was ready to lie down on those tracks. I could not break my yearlong lease without paying for the remaining months. In addition, this manager did not record my rent properly and when she was replaced by a new manager, I learned my rent was in arrears! This had never happened before, since that was the very first thing I took care of every month.

The new manager corrected the error. I liked him. He enforced the regulations and kept up the cleanliness of the building. Near the end of the year as I looked for a quieter place to live, my application was rejected because it was recorded on my credit record that I had not paid my rent on time! When the accountant had erroneously reported the initial rental payments as late, she failed to notify the credit agency after the correction was made. I had to request a statement clearing my record. In all my years of renting, I had never had management make such egregious errors, and that only to be repeated in my next apartment. No landlord will believe a tenant over previous management despite a lifetime of perfect rental payments.

The next year, I found a place away from the tracks, on Hague Avenue where the building sign touted professional management. When I moved in, the apartment, though promised to be clean, wasn't. Crusty oven, soiled floors, mold on bathroom tiles, a broken window. I objected strenuously because I had just left my previous apartment spotless, even taking out the windows to wash them. I had passed that inspection with flying colors only to be met with this. Since my mover was scheduled for the next day, the manager told me to deduct $20 per hour for cleaning the floors, and with pressure on my part, hired someone to clean the rest. In a few weeks she was replaced by a new manager. Over a year later, this new manager accused me of not paying my full rent for the month from which I had deducted the cleaning fee! Fortunately, I had written a note on my check and was able to exonerate myself.

The common areas of this building were seldom vacuumed in their entirety. Stains from large leaking plastic bags trailed from one end of the hall to the other. In the stairwells, cobwebs held the ninety-six-year-old building together. At one time it had been a beautiful building, but now the once lustrous window sills were rain damaged with no attempt made to restore the wood.

On the bright side, the entry windows always sparkled. The newspapers were promptly picked up, sometimes before we could read them. To her credit, the new manager eventually evicted the most offending tenants. Some strewed the halls with lint from the laundry or other debris and rang our doorbells in the middle of the night. I disconnected mine. The woman across the hall set out a huge black bag of garbage, and left it there for days at a time. When she did take it out, she placed it next to the trash bin. By morning the squirrels got at it, strewing about its contents. Over the years, was management getting more lax, or was I getting fussier?

The good part about this building was it had skilled and responsible maintenance men. Plumbing and electrical work was always done promptly and well. To balance this good fortune, the building also had mice. My friends who owned a farm lent me a mousetrap which I set the night I received it. Bam! At three o'clock in the morning it captured its prey.

Just before Christmas, a squirrel squeezed into the apartment through the flue above the stove. Now experienced in squirrel eviction, I encouraged the fat thing down three flights of stairs, and held the front door wide open. The varmint toyed with me, stood there staring at me as if debating whether or not to go out. Should he give up a warm and cozy building for his freedom? After much pleading and clicking of tongue, I watched it prance out in style as if to say, "I'm going because I want to, not because you want me to."

So far in my apartment life, I have evicted two squirrels, two bats, one pigeon, and one mouse, (but not yet a partridge in a pear tree). I was sorry to leave the place; it was like having pets without paying a pet fee. The rooms were spacious with lovely woodwork. Lovely that is, after I had removed paint drips, filled in the gouges, and touched it up perfectly with my oil paints. Truly, I would have stayed there, but the building was sold and the rent doubled. Best part was, my unit was used as the display model for prospective buyers. Before I moved out, I reported a chewing sound in the ceiling in the bathroom. No action was taken. I reported it twice more. The day I was leaving, a squirrel had gnawed right through.

As for living in buildings for people over fifty-five, I've tried them twice now, in two different cities, thinking there would be dear, kind old souls living there. But no. Gossip was rampant, there was shouting in hallways and walls so thin you could hear grandmothers screaming at their grandchildren through two sets of closed doors. Car doors slammed from midnight to 3 a.m. I presumed the only quiet place I would find would be my grave.

Luckily, not true! After three years, I found a quiet top floor apartment with only four other tenants on it. There is so much light that my orchid has forty-three blossoms on only one of its two spikes. Since the unit faces west, there are sunsets tempered by clouds that display a different arrangement of color each evening. At the end of the hall is a balcony from which I can view the sunrise from fall 'til spring. In summer I can see the tops of trees, some of which look like broccoli from that vantage point.

As I write this, the Covid-19 pandemic rages. Unable to visit my friends, I have made friends with the clouds. Never before have I witnessed such a variety of configurations.

5

My New York Experience

I had always wanted to pursue a degree of master of fine arts. In 1992, when I was fifty, I decided that since in two years I would be fifty-two with or without the degree, it was time to matriculate at the New York Graduate School of Figurative Art. My friends hoorayed me and more than a few came to visit me during my time there.

Following the advice of a friend who told me never to be seen reading a tourist guidebook on the street or appear as if I didn't know where I was going, I took the cover off the paperback *Book of English Literature* and glued it to my guidebook. I read that "English Lit" book as I walked around the same block four times, surreptitiously glancing at the street signs to get my bearings.

I was so thrilled to be in New York that as I was about to cross a side street, the light turned, but I, with my head in the clouds, crossed anyway. The traffic had already lurched forward and a man on a motorcycle stopped short in front of me with a "Christ, lady!"

When I visited the farmers market at Union Square, you can imagine my surprise when I saw weeds for sale as flowers—weeds such as bladder campion and hoary alyssum that I had pulled out of my father's fields on our midwestern farm.

I went roller skating in Central Park without giving much thought to how I would stop as I approached Columbus Circle. Luckily for me, there was a little rise just before the path ended, or my New York experience would have come to a premature end.

Attending the academy was heaven on earth: painting and drawing and creating sculptures all day, every day, one couldn't help but improve. It was like a full time dream job. We studied cadavers at Hunter College with a consultant from the medical field, who taught us the origin, function, and insertion of every muscle of the human body.

On Fridays, after returning from classes at 4 p.m., I slept till midnight and then went out dancing with my twenty-year-old classmates. The music was so loud, I put cotton balls in my ears. My new friends teased me, saying that anyone who had to put cotton in their ears shouldn't be out dancing. Every place of entertainment stayed open until 4 a.m.

During orientation, I put aside my initial plan of staying in the dorm at the New School of Research; a mistake, I was to find out. A woman from Texas invited me to share a one bedroom apartment on the Lower East Side. A band set up on Saturday night on a nearby rooftop and played from one 'til three. People parked their cars with doors wide open to play tooth-loosening amps. Small children were out with their parents well after midnight. Perhaps they were in training for "the city that never sleeps."

My roommate and I agreed the rent would be divided according to the space we used. She took the large bedroom, and I set up in the hallway. She said we would settle the rent proportionally after the first month. At the second month she asked if I had paid my rent. Having conscientiously paid it a few days in advance, I brought up the issue of proportionate rent. She informed me that she had changed her mind and the rent would not be adjusted. I had also foolishly paid the phone bill in advance.

The very next day, a Monday, I reserved a room at a women's residence on the Upper West Side. Then I went straight to the rental office and said that I had paid my rent with the wrong check from my Midwest account, which had insufficient funds. I showed her a check from my New York account with the amount filled out. The young woman went to the safe to get my first check, and sat down to look at it. A moment was suspended in time. I snatched it out of her hand

and ran out the door, both checks in hand, with her "Hey, you can't do that!" wafting after me.

Since it was a school day, I skipped classes, hired a mover, and packed up my belongings. By the time my roommate returned from classes in the afternoon, I had settled into my new place on the Upper West Side. I was unable to slip the key under the door when I left, so I went back to the apartment that evening to return it. That was a mistake. I should have thrown it in the East River. She, a minister's wife, tried to throw me to the floor. I wrapped my arm around the freestanding shelving holding her dishes, clock, radio, and knickknacks. The more she shoved me, the more the shelves quaked as some of the items teetered to the edge. She let go and shouted, "I don't want you ever to speak to me again!" I disappeared out the building and wondered why I would ever *want* to speak to her again, but she said it first, so she had the satisfaction.

The women's residence was fine, except it was run by a religious group that hired people who were recovering something-or-others with less than stellar administrative skills except for rent collection. A common bathroom was at the end of the hall. There was a resident on our floor who, in the midst of winter, opened the window wide whenever anyone was in the shower. There was another woman who always gave me a hard time on the elevator, demanding to know why I was going up when she wanted to go down.

I thought, "You're supposed to be creative. Figure out a way to live inexpensively in NYC." When the spring semester neared its end, I put up fliers on Fifth, Madison, and Park Avenues announcing that I was searching for a space to rent for the fall semester. Presuming that New Yorkers assume midwesterners are naïve and trustworthy, I listed both my New York and Minnesota phone numbers to improve my chances. While it was illegal to post signs on street lamps, I knew that thousands of people would pass by and read them before they were torn down. When I checked the posts the next morning, sure enough, all the fliers had been removed. But no matter. The offers started coming in, and as they say, truth is stranger than fiction.

Very quiet, older female, graduate student wants quiet, clean room or efficiency for '93-94 school year.

Please call: Theresa Tanta

Day: (212) 505- x x x x

Eve. & weekends: (212) 496- xxxx } *Before May 14*

Please leave message if I'm not in.

—

After May 14: (612) 225- xxx (Minnesota)

The flyer that got me a free place to live in Manhattan.

My first response was from "David Smith" who said his real name was Mike Quatrecelli, that he was a former hair stylist and most recently a gemstone cutter for Cartier's. Since business was slow he was considering returning to the barber business. He invited me to see his "gorgeous penthouse on the Upper West Side with its terrace and beautiful plants." It turned out to be a sty. A mangy cat greeted me at the door of the filthy living room. The couch in the living room facing the entrance door was what he had to offer for $500 a month. Outside, a very narrow terrace was strewn with roofing material among broken plastic containers with plants straggling out of them.

Never mind. Mike talked about himself constantly: his trips to India, his rapport with the Dali Lama, and his thirty days of absolute silence in a Trappist monastery. I did not tell him of my twenty-two years of experience in meditation. He showed me portfolios of photos and newspaper articles of his Cartier gemstone carvings. Truthfully, the work was outstanding; Faberge-like in some instances. Next out came 1970s magazines with photos of his hairstyling days; photos of himself styling Bob Hope's and Elvis Presley's hair. Finally, he gave a tour of his workshop with its amazing array of tiny custom-made gem-cutting tools, but primarily a room full of junk. Some tools were familiar to me from a jewelry class I had taken fifteen years earlier. As I left, he said, "At least you looked at it; the other two girls wouldn't even step in."

The most incredulous offer came from a man who presented himself as a friend of a hospitalized woman. I arrived at the designated location a few doors up from where the gemstone-cutter lived and met the man at the doorway. He introduced himself also as a "Michael." He said that the woman whose apartment he was showing was in the hospital with a tracheotomy and would be there for a month, but that he had a letter in her handwriting on hospital letterhead giving him permission to show her apartment. He showed me the pasted up copied letter and said he was doing this as a favor to her. The alarm bells sounded in my head, but I wanted to see where this would lead.

He said the last person who had rented the now available apartment had been stealing the woman's paintings. The woman's name was Santee Rose, he now informed me, and she had lived in the building for twenty years. But before he could show the space, he said we must go to the police department a couple of blocks away to get permission and a police escort to enter the apartment. Am I on *Candid Camera*? I wondered. We arrived at the station and he showed "the letter." No dice. Back to the building we went, but the doorman wouldn't let us in despite Michael's presentation of the letter. Nice lobby, I thought. Michael called the building owner on the entry phone and was placed on hold. We waited and waited. I excused myself and ran down a few blocks to copy transcripts for a job application. This was taking longer than was worth the entertainment. Michael was afraid I wouldn't return, but I did.

He then said he was going to discuss this with some character on cable TV who helped people in these situations and said I should call the following day. When I did, he said Santee was out of the hospital and I should call her in the afternoon at a number he had given me. Shortly thereafter, I received a call from a Michael Quatrinto (not to be confused with Michael Quatrecelli, the gemstone cutter, or the Michael who gave me the run-around to begin with) who asked me what the condition of the apartment was. He informed me the rent had been in arrears for some time. I told him I had never seen it and gave him the story. He said, "These things go on all the time." The whole thing was too hot to touch.

Many years later I read an article in the *New Yorker* about a man who took 42 down payments on the same apartment in Manhattan. The scam came to light when the would-be tenants began showing up at the same time. His name was Michael!

I began visiting additional apartments. A woman from California, had a small room to let. She said her name was Bond. Jane Bond. She was picky about where to meet—a bit wary, no doubt. Finally it was decided that we would meet at Bushy's on Madison Avenue. Jane was petite, wore a black velvet cloche over her curly shoulder-length hair, a black coat, and a beautiful shawl. She looked to be in her sixties despite false eyelashes, lavish mascara, and, by her own admission, a face-lift. Although eccentric, she was bright, articulate, and entertaining, talking constantly. Finally she invited me to her apartment to show the room, a room filled with objects d'art from floor almost to ceiling, and walls lined end to end with furniture; in short, a storage room. It would be $500 with no space for me to fit.

Then there was the place in Greenwich Village. The woman ran a graphic design service out of the apartment and offered her tiny, narrow foyer for the now ubiquitous $500. All of her clients entered her office through this foyer. A narrow cot against the wall made it even narrower.

A few days later, a woman called to say I could rent her son's place in Midtown, because he was a salesman who traveled all over the country and was almost never home. There was a condition: I would have to tell the residents that I was his girlfriend since they were not allowed to sublet apartments.

Then a professor who was home only on weekends said he would be happy to let his apartment. Another man called to say he had an extra bedroom, but he would have to walk through it to use the bathroom. Next, I agreed to meet with a tall, imposing Egyptian man who called himself "The Maestro." I took one look at him and walked in the opposite direction.

Finally, Janet, a widow at a penthouse on the Upper East Side between Madison and Fifth, called me for an interview. She was petite and savvy with a good sense of humor. She offered, free of charge, a private bedroom and tiny bath with use of the kitchen, dining room, and spacious living room. In exchange, I would prepare two meals a week, water the plants on the terrace, and run errands. I could easily see the Guggenheim from her terrace. The bathroom fixtures were so arranged that I'd have to reach over the toilet to access the sink. Never mind, I was satisfied that I had secured a place for the fall semester.

During the interview with Janet I expressed surprise that she would accept me, not knowing me outside my Midwest references. "I'm surprised you would want to live with *me*, considering my last name is Berkowitz," she countered. The reference was to the "Son of Sam" serial killer active in those days. Her late husband, an attorney for a major entertainment corporation, had forfeited a promotion because he refused to shorten his name to "Berk." I was surprised to learn that anti-Semitism was still alive and well.

The second weekend after I arrived, Janet hired a car to take her to Old Greenwich in Connecticut, leaving me alone in her penthouse. I was astonished at her trust level. Equally surprising was that at eighty-two, she often went out on the town with her friends after ten p.m. for a performance of some sort. That was the hour I dropped my exhausted fifty-one-year-old self into bed and fell asleep.

Janet's furniture was original Eero Saarinen, Herman Miller, Bertoia and Fratinni, and Jehs and Laub. The pieces were not knock-offs. There was an original mottled shag rug which had to be combed with a special wooden rake. This was done by the cleaning woman from Belize after she had vacuumed. Janet's dining room was hung with original paintings of Milton Avery, Robert Motherwell, Robert Rauschenberg, and Sam Francis. There was also a signed informal photograph of Picasso with her husband and herself.

Five fur coats hung in Janet's entrance closet. One had narrow strips of fur alternating with gold grosgrain ribbon. When the weather turned cold, she twice offered to let me wear any of them. I declined.

We got along well. Once I picked up a placemat from Planet Hollywood and put it on her tray when I served her dinner in her room. Janet got a kick out of that. She enjoyed my homemade egg dumplings, and I enjoyed having a clean, quiet place in an upscale environment. She often let me use her year-round ticket to the Metropolitan Museum of Art, where I sat for hours contemplating Thomas Cole's painting, "The Oxbow," the Greek kouroi, and Mastata, Tomb of Pernel. As a tourist, one tends to rush from one gallery to another without the luxury of such leisure.

During the fall semester the first bombing at the World Trade Center building took place. I heard the explosions as I was picking up art supplies at Pearl Paint on Pearl Street. That night television reception was almost impossible since eight million New Yorkers, hungry for news, were tuning in.

Since the Academy was in Tribeca, I had to take the subway through Times Square during rush hour. It was always packed—standing room only. I held my wet oil paintings over my head and cautioned,

Janet took my photo while I lived at her penthouse on 88th St. in New York.

"Careful, these paintings are wet." A halo of space opened around me.

I learned to get on the train when it was nearly full so I could hop off without getting caught in the throngs. I was so adept at hopping off that one evening I outdid myself. The doors closed immediately behind me, which prevented additional passengers from exiting while also preventing me from hopping back on. Something was going on. I stood stone still and slap flat against the train while my eyes counted twenty-one police officers swarming the station. They soon caught their man and cuffed him. The station emptied, the train doors opened again, and since I was still alive, I far outstripped the crowd.

I became so familiar with the subway system that tourists began to ask me which was the local train and which the express. I began to feel like an intrepid New Yorker. Sometimes a garbled announcement was made while on the express stating that from this point on, this train would be a local. A friend from Minnesota was visiting once when that happened. "How can they do that?" he asked. "This is New York," I answered.

But eventually the stimulation of the Big City began to wear me down. In January, exhausted after a long evening studio class, I tried to out-walk the bitter cold on my way to the Tribeca subway station. A hale and hearty panhandler extended his hand and barked: "Got a quarter?" "Do I look like I have a quarter?" I retorted. Big mistake. "Do you think it's easy standing out here in the cold?" he challenged me. "It might be easier to get a job," was my unverbalized thought. I had never moved so quickly down those subway stairs.

Every morning, my penthouse landlady tripped into the kitchen in her heeled silver slippers, peripatetically crossing the slightly raised threshold. Considering Janet's advanced age, I cringed, and sometimes came close to cautioning her against wearing those little heels.

One February morning, the inevitable happened. Janet misjudged the width of the threshold and fell to the floor, fracturing her collarbone. Broke it clear through at age eighty-two. Upon her return from emergency care, in moved a private nurse, and out the door went my expendable self.

After I graduated and returned to the Midwest, we corresponded and I once went back to New York to visit Janet, bringing her some real Challah bread with walnuts and raisins from the Lower East Side. Shortly thereafter, Janet died. Interestingly, she once told me that she and her childless friends, widowed or single, had an unwritten pact that their jewelry be distributed among one another upon the death of any of them. I often wondered how that panned out, for she had some beautiful pieces.

The February move was not convenient, since I had sent out a huge resume mailing. This all took place before personal computers were commonplace. I had a service transfer calls to my new address until I left in May. I had expected all of these universities to be clamoring (*clamas, clamat clamant*) to hire me by then. After sending out 511 resumes with slides of my artwork, I began receiving replies suggesting they meant what they said when they had requested two years of university level teaching experience. None of my teaching and art degrees counted, nor did my experience conducting adult art classes, seminars, and workshops.

I then moved into a room in a fifth floor walk-up on York Avenue next to Casey's Dance Hall and Saloon. I had fallen from high places, so to speak, but it was on the top floor so I could see the sky every morning. There were many five-story buildings because by law, if a building had more floors than that, it was required to have a water tank. Janet's leaked while I was with her and caused damage to her ceilings. My new room was located near Gracie Mansion and the lovely Carl Schurz Park by the East River.

The room was sublet by a Brazilian woman, Cecilia, and her twelve-year-old daughter, Jessica. Five floors up, she had of all things, a stairstep exercise machine. Often when returning from school, I stopped at a bodega to pick up a pint of coffee-flavored Häagen-Dazs ice cream. When I approached the bottom of the apartment stairs, I contemplated whether it would be easier to carry it in my hand or my stomach.

Casey's remained open until four a.m. as is the custom for bars in New York. As the drunken patrons left the bar, they often honked their car horns wildly. Once, during the cacophony, the Brazilian woman threw eggs down on those cars.

Then, as everyone in New York knows, after the bars quieted down, the garbage trucks came by.

Living with a twelve-year-old proved to be entertaining. Jessica fell in the street one day across from a fire station. The fire fighters promptly took her to the hospital by ambulance. Her tongue stuck out of her mouth as she fell, and as she later put it, "I licked the streets of New York." She was not injured except for a slight scrape on each of the high points of her face. Her mother informed her that her trip to the hospital was the most expensive ride she would ever have: $250

(left) Graduation day at the New York Graduate School of Figurative Art when I received my master's degree of Fine Art on May 15, 1994.

(above and below) My dearest friends, Laurie and Dick, came to New York all the way from Moorhead, MN, to celebrate my graduation!

for six blocks. "You could get a helicopter ride over the 'cee-ty' for $60," she reminded her daughter.

When I broke Cecilia's glass baking dish, I replaced it with a similar one. I apologized that it was not identical. She was surprised that I had replaced it at all and smiled. This served me in good stead after graduation when a major package shipping company twice failed to pick up my boxes of belongings. She managed the pick-up after I left town. I had sweetened the pot by giving her a large oil sketch I had made of her daughter.

For my graduation, my friends came all the way from Moorhead, Minnesota, to celebrate with me. We walked the Brooklyn Bridge, took the ferry to Staten Island, and enjoyed the Cloisters in Harlem.

On May 30, I turned fifty-two, with the degree.

6

Fullfillment

Hold fast to dreams,
For if dreams die
Life is a broken-winged bird
That cannot fly.

– Langston Hughes

In 1994, upon returning from New York with my newly minted degree, my priority was to become financially solvent. My former manager wanted me back at my old social services job where my responsibility was to provide training for older dislocated workers. How lucky, yet what irony! I had arrived on May 28 and my supervisor wanted me to start work on June 1. My packages from New York had not yet arrived, and except for my luggage, the rest of my belongings were in storage. "Please," I begged her, "may I have a day off to get my car out of storage, obtain license tabs, pass the pollution test, and get a tune-up?"

So it was a daily commute from Saint Paul to Minneapolis on the I-94 killer freeway, now four lanes of bumper-to-bumper traffic since alternate freeways were undergoing repairs. One solution was to leave for work at 6:30 a.m. But what to do when I arrived at my destination so early? I decided to roller-skate around the lake 'til the office opened. In my opinion, roller-skating is the next best thing to

Oils, clockwise from upper left: *Woman in Thought, The Violinist, Woman Gazing Out Her Window, Candlelight.*

Oils, clockwise from upper left: *Victoria, Peony in Light, Andrew, Peonies III.*

flying. I was dying to paint, but for the time being I was preoccupied with apartment hunting and the five hours of computer training per week that my position now required. Microsoft Windows had come on the market while I was in New York and I needed to catch up. In the meantime, a friend graciously let me a room in her condominium at the Commodore in Saint Paul, where I had rented an apartment before moving to New York. I began to paint after work and on weekends. Spare moments were spent reconnecting with friends.

When the state cut the budget for my position, I was hired for the same type of job at another venue. It was here that I had a client with the name of "Buick." I couldn't believe it. Once, when I was very young, I saw the chrome emblem on the radiator of a Buick. I became so enamored of the look of the chrome logo on its dark blue ground and with the sound of the word, that I vowed when I had a daughter, I would name her "Buick." Now, more than forty-eight years later, the name had actually surfaced!

It was a decent job and I would have stayed there indefinitely while painting "on the side," but after a year, I injured my back. The result was four bulging discs, one of them ruptured; I could not sit without acute pain. Soon after, the state cut the budget for my position. I had no option but to apply for disability payments. It was a lengthy process and required using up monies in my 403K and 401K retirement plans. I was deeply embarrassed, for despite my desperate situation, I felt I was mooching off the government. I applied to a program to become self-employed by producing and selling my paintings. One of the program requirements was to apply for grants to supplement my income. I had never done this before, thinking my work would not qualify. To my surprise and delight, I won several awards including some for $3,000 and $4,000.

I wrote a business plan and researched supply companies. The advantage of being self-employed was that I could stand rather than sit, take frequent breaks, apply ice packs when necessary, and perform thirteen physical therapy exercises three times a day, as recommended by my physician. As debilitating as this was, it was not the first time my body had betrayed me. I accepted this latest setback as a part of life and this time did not imagine it was the end of the world. I didn't complain much about the pain because it's tiresome to listen to such laments; and listening to myself complain just made me feel worse. Instead, I accepted every invitation I received to dine out, even if it meant kneeling at the restaurant table.

I rented wine glasses by the dozen and made my own hors d'oeuvres. People volunteered to assist during the exhibitions and some even brought a bottle of wine or contributed appetizers. Some

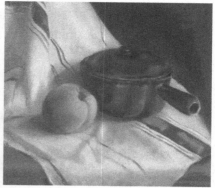

Oils: (left) *Pears with a Ginger Jar;* (right) *Peach with Blue Pot.*

of my neighbors offered their beautiful Victorian homes for my exhibitions. Local organizations viewed my exhibits as community events and did not charge me for ads I placed in their newsletters. In the course of time I developed a mailing list of almost two-thousand names. And every year I donated a painting to the silent auction held at the Ramsey Hill Neighborhood Association in Saint Paul.

Eventually I was earning enough by selling my paintings to get off disability. I did not make it known that I was unable to work a regular job. I wanted people to purchase my work because they liked it, not out of pity. As my sales increased, so did my confidence. I began entering competitions nationwide and was pleasantly surprised when my paintings were accepted. Several of my paintings were chosen for juried exhibitions and private collections in New York, Boca Raton, New Orleans, Chicago, London, Germany, Malaysia, and other far-flung places. My burgeoning national reputation expanded my credibility and greatly increased my local sales. After all, "What good can come out of Nazareth?"

Patrons invited me to dinner to show where they had displayed my paintings. Often a friendship evolved. A woman from Chicago purchased one of my paintings from a gallery in Sanibel Island in Florida, and grew to like it so much that she took a road trip to St. Paul with her children to see more of my work. At the time I was living in Frogtown. I rushed to pick up the trash on the streets before they arrived. The woman bought two more paintings and generously offered the free use of her guest house on Captiva Island. She even gave me her frequent flyer miles for the trip and told me to invite two friends to join me!

After having worked at corporations and small businesses, at for-profits and non-profits, in education, graphic design, and social work, I had finally reached my stride running my own business as an artist. Staff meetings took one minute. Should I do this? Yes. Any discussion? No. I taught myself how to use Quicken, which made accounting a breeze.

Using my telemarketing experience, I cold called prospective galleries I had researched. The hard part was the mental shift from creating art to marketing it, and then back again. All the skills I had learned in past occupations converged to make my marketing successful to the point where

Oils: (top) *Araucana Eggs;* (bottom) *Oranges in Conversation.*

I actually enjoyed it. In fact, it became difficult to keep up with the production of the art itself. An example of this occurred when the Stricoff Fine Art Gallery of New York verbally accepted one of my large paintings, but then dropped it from the exhibition because I didn't have a body of work to accompany it. It was a great disappointment because it was a good gallery and I was trying to build a New York reputation.

I also continued freelancing while painting. My most lucrative assignment was from Morgan Stanley, an investment bank in New York. This was just before 9/11.

Watercolors, clockwise from upper left: *Christmas Tête-à-tête; Amarylis; Bethesda Fountain in Central Park, N.Y.; Pegee Hydrangeas.*

Patrons began requesting commissions, something I had not at all expected. At first I accepted every commission offered because it was guaranteed income with which to pay the rent. Besides, it was flattering. But as the orders mounted, I soon had little or no time to paint my own work. This began to encroach upon my ability to produce my own art and I feared I would lose the spirit of painting originals.

Those who liked figurative works for which I had trained in New York, often went on to buy several at a time. Most liked the still lifes and florals. I characterize my works as "isles of silence, stillness and light in a time of noise, talk and activity; they are catalysts of tranquility for the spirit."

Galleries wanted bodies of work, which tied up a good part of my inventory, taking it off the local market until a given show was over. I had to document my work by having slides made of each piece, record the relevant information for future reference, sign contracts and fill out application forms. I needed to order and assemble frames for the paintings and print labels with titles, dimensions, and prices. Sometimes it took the entire day to pack a large painting and ship it to its destination. Along the way I learned an important rule of thumb: do not market more than you can deliver.

Most galleries want an artist statement to accompany an entry. To this day I do not understand the need for a statement. The painting *is* the statement. Isn't a picture worth a thousand words? If an artist statement is so important, why aren't bestselling authors required to paint a picture to illustrate their books?

Many prospective patrons asked, "How long did it take you to paint that?" The question was unanswerable because my painting time was often interrupted by inquiries from galleries and prospective clients. Because I sometimes worked on several paintings at once, it was virtually impossible to keep track of the time. Furthermore, once I started painting I lost the sense of time. This is known as "the flow" or being in "the zone." One paints the feeling. It is expressed in imagery in shape, form, color, value, and composition.

These years were the fulfillment of a dream I had nurtured from a very young age. My guiding light was a quotation of Goethe:

> "*Until one is committed, there is hesitancy, the chance to draw back. Concerning all acts of initiative (and creation), there is one elementary truth that ignorance of which kills countless ideas and splendid plans: that the moment one definitely commits oneself, then Providence moves too. All sorts of things occur to help one that would never otherwise have occurred. A whole stream of events issues from the decision, raising in one's favor all manner of unforeseen incidents and meetings and material assistance, which no man could have dreamed would have come his way. Whatever you can do, or dream you can do, begin it. Boldness has genius, power, and magic in it. Begin it now.*"

Artist Vita

Theresa Wanta, BSE, BFA, MFA

Artist Awards

Christopher Reeve Foundation, Springfield, New Jersey 2004
VSA Grant (Jerome Foundation), St. Paul, Minnesota 1998, 2001
E.D. Foundation Grant, Kearney, New Jersey 2000
National Finalist: Honors, The Artist's Magazine 1991
State: First Place, Minnesota United Way Communications 1987
State: Second Place, University of Wisconsin System, Excellence in
    Visual Communications 1986
Local: PEO Sisterhood Award, Stevens Point, Wisconsin 1982
Local: Second Place, "Women Creating", Charles M.White
    Memorial Public Library, Stevens Point, Wisconsin 1981

Selected Juried Exhibitions

Visions XI, Riverfront Arts Center, Stevens Point, Wisconsin 2013-14
Owatonna Arts Center, Owatonna, Minnesota 2004
Minneapolis Foundation, Minneapolis, Minnesota 2003
University of Minnesota, Coffman Building 2003
New York Academy of Art, New York, New York 1992, 94, 02
The Art Source, Indianapolis, Indiana 2002
Ariana Gallery, Royal Oak, Michigan 1999-2000
Unity Unitarian Gallery, Saint Paul, MN 2000
The Art Collector's Gallery, Solana Beach, California 1999
Susan Street Gallery, San Diego, California 1999
"Dialogues with Visual Tradition"; Philip Pearlstein, Juror; New York
    Academy of Art, New York 1998
Schoharie County Arts Council National Small Works, Cobleskill,
    New York 1998
Downey Museum of Art, Downey, California 1997-8
Jacob Javits Federal Building, New York, New York 1995
J. Michael Gallery, Minneapolis, Minnesota 1990
Northern Watercolor Society, Saint Paul, Minnesota 1990
Edna Carlston Gallery, University of Wisconsin-Stevens Point 1980

Selected Exhibitions

ArtsWalk, Stevens Point, Wisconsin 2011

St. Paul Art Crawl, Saint Paul, Minnesota 2001-2007

Cloister Gallery, House of Hope, Saint Paul, Minnesota 1998, 2006

Studio Exhibitions, Saint Paul, Minnesota 1994-2006

University Club of Saint Paul, Minnesota 2003

Harriet Barry Gallery, University of Wisconsin-River Falls, 2003

Ecolab Corporation, Saint Paul, Minnesota 2002

Vision Loss Resources Gallery, Minneapolis, Minnesota 2002

Waterfall Gallery, Government Center, Minneapolis, Minneota 2002

Dragonfly Gallery, Stockholm, Wisconsin 2001

Foxworthy's, Sanibel Island, Florida 1998-99

Small Works Exhibition, Cobleskill, New York 1998

SoHo Gallery, Pensacola, Florida 1997-8

Art Showcase, New York, New York 1997

Stockholm Gallery, Stockholm, Wisconsin 1992-3, 96-97

Caesarea Gallery, Boca Raton, Florida 1995-6

Suzanne Kohn Gallery, Saint Paul, Minnesota 1992-3

Saint Paul Gallery, Saint Paul, Minnesota 1991-92

The Commodore, Saint Paul, Minnesota 1991

The Other Foot In the Door Show, Minneapolis Institute of Art,
   Minnesota 1990

The Red Geranium, Magnolia House, Houma, Louisiana 1975

Private Collections

London, Germany, Kuala Lumpur; New York City, Washington, D.C.,
Philadelphia, Boston, Boca Raton, New Orleans, Chicago, West
   Coast, Midwest

Freelance Trainer and Speaker

Art Appreciation Presentations, Dayton's Bluff Public Library, Saint
   Paul, Minnesota 2019

Marketing Your Art, Continuing Education, University of Wisconsin
   2010-11

VSA at University of Minnesota, Minneapolis, Minnesota 1998

HIRED, Minneapolis, Minnesota 1991-82

Want-A-Workshop: Workshops in Art, Minneapolis, Minnesota 1990-91

Artsign Workshops, Minneapolis, Minnesota 1989-90
Minnesota Museum of American Art, Saint Paul, Minnesota 1990
Burnsville Community Center, Burnsville, Minnesota 1990
Open University, Minneapolis, Minnesota 1989
Associated Seminars, Minneapolis, Minnesota 1989
Northwestern National Life Insurance Company, Minneapolis,
    Minnesota 1985
Department of Art Education, University of Wisconsin-Stevens Point 1982
Department of Fine Arts, University of Wisconsin-Stevens Point 1982
Freelance Seminars, University of Wisconsin-Stevens Point 1981-2
Resident Training and Counseling Program, University of Wisconsin-
    Stevens Point 1979-80
Adult Community Education, Houma, Louisiana 1974-5
In-service Teacher Training, Green Bay, Wisconsin 1972-3
In-service Training for Instructors, Oshkosh, Wisconsin 1969
Art Instruction, Milwaukee, Wisconsin, 1968-69

Education
Master of Fine Arts: New York Academy of Art: Graduate School of
    Figurative Art, New York, NY, 1994
Bachelor of Fine Arts in Art: University of Wisconsin-Stevens Point,
    with honors, 1982
Bachelor of Science in Education: St. Norbert College, Depere,WI,
    with honors, 1969

Selected Coursework
Art Student League of New York, NY 1982, 1986
Fashion Institute of Technology, New York, NY 1986
Atelier Lack, Minneapolis, MN 1986, 1987, 1989
University of Minnesota, MN 1985-1986, 1988, 1989
Parsons School of Design, New York, NY 1982
Minneapolis College of Art and Design, Minneapolis, MN 1983
Art and Architecture of Russia, Soviet Seminar, Russia 1981

Selected Workshops
"Making Color Sing." Jean Dobie (Philadelphia) Banfill-Locke Art
    Center, Minneapolis, Minnesota 1991

"Portrait Painting." Daniel Green (New York), Minneapolis, Minnesota 1990

"Figure Drawing." Judith Roode, Split Rock, Duluth, Minnesota 1990

"Artist Business Classes." United Arts Council, St. Paul, Minnesota, 1985

"Design Methods." Dynamic Graphics Seminar, Chicago, Illinois 1982

"Exploring Watercolor." University of Wisconsin Extension, Rhinelander, Wisconsin 1979

7

Origins

My maternal great-great-grandfather, Michael Von Kozicz-kowski, was a Polish nobleman of the landed gentry from the Kasubian district of Karthaus in the province of West Prussia, in the area of Gdansk (or Danzig, depending on who controlled Poland). He spoke French, Polish, German, Latin, and English. The Kingdom of Prussia, as a member of the German Confederation (from 1815 to 1866), taxed his property to the point where he had to sell more and more of it to come up with the payments. Recognizing that eventually, there would be no inheritance left for his children, he and his family immigrated to the United States in 1857, on the German ship *Howard.* This was fortuitous because Prussia became part of the German Empire in 1871 under Bismarck, and the government initiated the Prussian deportations between 1885 and

Michael Von Koziczkowski, first Polish settler of Portage County.

1890. While some emigrants who moved to America saw it as an opportunity to add a title to their names, Michael dropped the "Von" part of his name when he arrived in America because he didn't think class distinction belonged in a democracy.

The Michael Koziczkowski Park in Stevens Point, Wisconsin, honors him as the first Polish settler in Portage County. My mother, Susan Domaszek, his great granddaughter, grew up on a farm near Polonia, Wisconsin. Her mother, Frances Koziczkowski, died in childbirth when my mother was five years old. Leo Domaszek, her father, remarried to Helen Dombeck.

Leo Domaszek, my maternal grandfather, was born to Julia Molski and Matthew Domaszek. My mother lists Matthew as being born in Gdansk, Koscierzyna, Poland. Julia died when my grandfather Leo was nine years old. "Domaszek" translates as "little home." Leo anglicized his name to Damask to enable his sons to find jobs because of discrimination against the Poles. One stubborn uncle who had a Popeye "I yam what I yam" mentality, reverted to the original name. I always admired him for that.

My paternal great-great grandparents, Andrew and Rozalie Landowski, departed for America in 1872 with six of their seven children on the "good ship Braunschweig." Rozalie died en route and was buried at sea. The ship put into port at Ellis Island in New York. My mother lists Andrew Landowski as born in Gdansk, Koscierzyna, Poland, and his wife Rozalie Wardni of unknown parentage. Oral tradition had it that she was of German descent. The name Landowski translates as "meadow land owner." Anton, born in Poland in 1856, and the youngest son of Andrew and Rozalie, married Pauline Piechowski in 1882. My grandmother, Anastasia, the oldest of their twelve children, married my grandfather John Wanta.

My paternal grandfather, John Wanta, (the name, an anglicized form of Wynta pronounced *vine ta* since the "w" is pronounced as a "v") was Polish, though no one can trace the actual name to Germany or Poland. It was also sometimes spelled or misspelled as "Wenta." John was born to Joseph and Katherine (Dallman) Wanta on Staten Island, New York. His parents emigrated from Prussian-occupied Poland, the Kasuby area south of Gdansk, or Danzig. He moved with his family to Portage County when he was five and married Anastasia Landowski in 1902. Since ancestors on both sides of my family came from the same area in Poland, it's a wonder they all didn't know each other before coming to America.

My father, Emil, the youngest of John and Stasia's thirteen children, (eight of whom died as infants or stillbirths, and one at age twenty-four) remained on the farm after he married my mother, and eventually bought it. My mother always said he never left home. Dad did not like to farm but was an excellent mechanic. He was happiest when he took on a job in winter delivering appliances with a buddy or overhauling cars or tractors. He could look at someone's flatbed, assess the length and width of the wood, and voila! He built one just like it. He enjoyed varied social situations, whereas my mother was more comfortable with relatives, especially her sisters.

Dad also enjoyed playing the concertina, which has a bright, crisp sound compared to the grinding drone of the accordion. He attended the same country school that I did later, but did not finish the sixth grade because he said the German teacher "had it in for" the Polish students. Historically there has long been an antipathy between Germans and Poles. He said that once this teacher hung a little boy by his suspenders on a clothes hook in the cloakroom because he was a slow learner, and that was it. He quit school.

My mother, the oldest in her family, liked the farm and saw the value of real estate. She attended elementary school until eighth grade but could write sentences with subject-verb agreement, used direct object pronouns correctly, and understood when and when not to use an apostrophe with an "s". She was good at math, and did the bookkeeping for the farm. She loved to read but had to shelve that desire because there was no time for it. My mother was the quintessential housewife, the term then used. She was an accomplished cook, seamstress, gardener and general manager. For many years, she enjoyed volunteering as sacristan at St. Agnes, our mission church a mile away.

My parents met at a church picnic, which was an annual fundraiser for the parish. Before her marriage, mother did housework in Wausau, Wisconsin, for the Sayers and for Grant Ford. The summer before she married she worked as a cook and nanny for Dr. Davey in Evanston, Illinois. It was the custom for farm girls to work in a larger city before they married.

(above) My mother before her marriage. (right) My parents' wedding picture, 1937.

I was born on a "dark and stormy night" just after midnight, on Memorial Day, in the middle of World War II. I never had to attend school on my birthday since this was long before Memorial Day was standardized to be observed on Mondays. My father drove my mother to St. Mary's hospital in Wausau, ten miles away. I was named for St. Theresa, but was never sure if it was of Lisieux or Avila. In those days,

Catholic children were often named for saints who were then considered their patrons. I chose Therese of Lisieux until I was twenty-four, the age she died. Then I switched to Theresa of Avila, a doctor of the church. Both were nuns. I was the third of five children, with two older sisters, a younger brother,

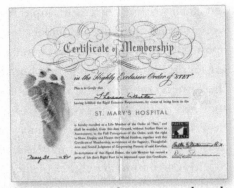

Complimentary document, though I was never able to determine what "STET" stood for.

and a youngest sister. Farmers always wanted sons who could help on the farm, but lacking sons, daughters always picked up the slack.

Our extended family included my paternal grandparents with whom we lived until we bought the farm from them in 1950. We ate meals together in the old part of the house where Grandma and Grandpa lived, and lived in the newer section. While we did not pay cash for rent, we paid it in kind with our labor.

We also shared my grandparents' visitors. Except for my maternal grandmother, who hugged us, we tended toward the European style of greeting by shaking hands. I observed from the periphery of the circle as Grandpa's brothers would visit and tell stories in Polish, which they called "boykas," slap their thighs, and laugh uproariously.

My grandfather told of the past, when the Ojibwe Indians asked for meat as they passed through the area. He always obliged. In return, they gave him hand-woven birch baskets of various sizes and shapes. As a child, I never paid much attention to those baskets because they were just always there. I liked best a small birchbark canoe that was used to store wooden matches; it hung high up on the gas lamp fixture, out of the reach of children.

My grandfather, John Wanta, told of walking to Kempster lumber camp in northern Wisconsin when he was a young man, a distance of roughly 150 miles. I can't imagine walking that far. In the early 1900s he purchased the farm under the Homestead Act for a dollar an acre. It was located nine miles east of Wausau on Highway 29. He built the house and out buildings, mostly by his own hand, but did not install electricity or plumbing. The barn was built of tamarack so it didn't need to be painted. The bottom portion was constructed of stones and cement in the European style.

I liked to observe my grandfather. He liked to eat with a table knife rather than a fork and slurp his coffee. Sometimes he poured some off into a saucer to cool it first. When he received mail, he always opened the envelope from one end with a table knife and blew into it to open it wider. I sat nearby hoping it was something he didn't want so I could use the backside of the letter for drawing pictures, since it didn't have lines as my tablet did. If it was an advertisement he would say, "All they want is my money," and toss it on the table, and I would pounce on it happily.

Aerial view of our farm, the buildings clockwise from left: barn, granary with machine sheds, garage hidden by elm tree, four square house with old part in front, toolshed with barely visible pig house attached in back and the outhouse in front. Under the elm tree sits the water tank, and next to it, the pig wallow. Near the center stands the main chicken coop, and in front of the house there appears but a portion of the extensive garden.

My grandfather liked me and laughed at my foibles. I followed him around the toolshed and watched him solder and pound red hot metal on the anvil to fabricate something or other. One summer afternoon I stood behind him as he sat in his rocking chair in the kitchen, with the breeze blowing through it from the front porch to the back porch. As he rocked back and forth, I held my little scissors and waited for just the right rhythm of the "back" to snip his sparse, snowy hair, which caught in the scissors on the "forth." He didn't scold me, but thought it was funny. Because we lived with these grandparents, I thought he was solely ours. When my cousins claimed him, too, I vehemently insisted he couldn't be *their* grandfather because he was *ours.*

When we were guests at someone else's house we had the custom of saying, "no" when asked if we would like something to eat or drink. Then the host would ask again, to which we replied with the same answer. After the third offer, we said "yes." It was considered impolite and greedy to respond affirmatively to the first offer. Once my Auntie

Clara, who made the best chocolate cherry cake, asked what I would like, to which I politely replied, "nothing." She said they didn't have any of that! As an adult, when the host offered refreshment, I refused, expecting a second offer. To my surprise, I didn't get another offer!

As a preschooler, I stuttered (in Polish) when I got so excited I couldn't get the words out. This drew scorn from my siblings, and they mocked me, but my grandfather found it entertaining and chuckled. Once when he returned by Greyhound bus from shopping in Wausau, he brought us bubble gum, which he called "splash gum." In Polish, which sounds funnier, I stuttered, "Ja-ja-ja *gryzę żutam.*" (I-I-I chewed it.) He thought it great entertainment and asked me to perform when relatives visited, which I eagerly did, relishing the attention. I felt close to this grandfather who had such a good sense of humor.

I know he favored me because when I started picking potatoes in first grade—only half days and after school—he paid me fifty cents at the end of the season. My sister in third grade had picked all day and received only twenty-five cents. My mother, seeing the injustice of it, insisted my grandfather exchange the amounts between us, but he refused, chuckling at my delight. Again she insisted; again he refused. I knew my mother was right, but was elated that he liked me so much. After he left the room, my mother made me exchange the amount with my sister. While it was true my sister had picked more hours than I had, I will not forget how the thrill of being so lucky was undermined by the dispensation of justice.

Both grandparents read Polish publications, some of them religious in nature. As an adult, long after they were deceased, I had the opportunity to illustrate mastheads for the months of the calendar for one of them, *The Franciscan Message.* My grandmother knit mittens, socks, and woolen gloves with a beautiful braid design on them. As itchy as they were, they really kept my hands warm, and I wish I had them today.

Though fifth-generation Poles, we defaulted into speaking Polish until my oldest sister began first grade and had trouble understanding the teacher, who, of course, spoke English. Suddenly my parents began speaking only English. By the time I began first grade three years later, I knew hardly any Polish. I tried to speak it with my grandmother who knew hardly any English. We tried very hard to pronounce our "th's" and wouldn't be caught dead saying "dese," "dem," or "dose," as some of our neighbors did. We wanted to be American.

Our social life revolved around church, school, and relatives. Our cousins—the geographically closest—lived only a few hundred yards away, and the most distant, 40 miles away. Some lived in Illinois, but that hardly counted since we never left the state.

Although the Rural Electrification Act passed in 1936, World War II interrupted its implementation. I worried about how I would do my homework during the dark winter evenings when I got to first grade until I observed my two older sisters doing homework by the light of the kerosene lamp. I also worried about where the pencil sharpener and wastebasket would be. In my small mind, those were essential to survival in school. Again, my fears were allayed when my sisters enlightened me before my first day.

Not only was school a great escape from manual labor, there I had access to books, and received praise for my work. I particularly enjoyed meeting children of Italian, Irish, English and German descent, because they were different from our Catholic, Polish, and mostly farm relatives. My mother cautioned me not to associate too much with non-Catholics.

For my first three years in school, I walked with my sisters—a round trip of three miles—to Upper Kelley, a one room school that had a wood burning stove but no running water, just like at home. But unlike my home, it did have electric lights. A woodshed stood behind the school from which the eighth grade boys brought in wood for the classic potbellied stove, which stood in the back of the room.

With fox fur collars turned up, we walked the distance every day unless the temperature was below zero; then we stayed home. Sometimes a neighbor offered a ride. Later we got central heating at school—an anomaly since there was only one room—and one day the furnace went out. So after arriving, we all had to walk back home.

Class of 1948-1949 in front of our school, Upper Kelly, in the Town of Weston. Six of the students are my relatives. I'm in first grade, seated in the second row, third from right. It was a beautiful spring day.

The schoolteacher, who wore nylon stockings, put mittens on her feet until all the children had arrived and left.

There were two front entrances to the one room school: a "Boys' Hall" located on the left and the "Girls' Hall" to the right. The girls' hall was mainly a cloakroom for the girls, while the boys' also held shelves of construction paper. Oh, the thrill of smelling the reams of white and colored construction paper, imagining all the potential those beautiful pieces of paper held for artwork!

Our water source, also in the boys' hall, was a copper water container with a spigot at the bottom that bubbled up as a drinking fountain. The "big boys"—seventh and eighth graders—drew water from a hand pump outside and carried it in to fill the copper container early in the school day and again at noon. This hall also had a sink, a mirror, and two rows of hooks along the wall for the boys' coats. I wondered on which hook my father saw his teacher hang the little boy by his suspenders.

The Palmer cursive alphabet bordered the top of the slate blackboard, just below the long, narrow cork board which stretched around the room. In the center of the front wall, above the cork board, hung a clock with Roman numerals. I learned to tell time on it, adding and subtracting the I's, V's, and X's before figuring out if they were minutes before or after the hour.

All the students did drawings while they listened to Dr. Schwabach's radio program, *Let's Draw*, and the best of them were displayed on the cork boards. I felt honored whenever one of my drawings was selected by the eighth grade girls. The Wisconsin School of the Air programs were transmitted from distant Auburndale, so we had to take turns holding our hand against the back of the radio to improve the reception. Other weekly programs we enjoyed were Professor Gordon's *Let's Sing, Book Trails*, and various news and science programs.

We paid for our own school supplies with the money we earned picking beans and potatoes. A new box of eight crayons smelled good and was more than satisfactory until we got to school and saw some students had 48 crayons. We bought a new tablet with the "Big Chief" name brand and the profile of an American Indian in a feathered headdress printed on the red cover. Inside were newsprint pages with blue lines. I liked the smell of its newness.

Sometimes, my dad gave us fifty cents for picking potato bugs off the bushes. These larvae were pinkish orange with tiny black dots on them. At other times, he paid us each seventy-five cents to pull particularly pesky weeds out of a field. Our neighbor farmer did not eliminate this weed which resulted in the seeds blowing into our field, so we named it "Stryj" after him, which means paternal uncle.

Even in first grade, I thought it was silly to have mittens attached to a string that went up the coat sleeves and around the back of the coat. I thought that was for babies. I could keep track of my own mittens. I carried my lunch to school in a tin two-quart Karo Syrup pail. When, many years later, I read Tom Brokaw's book, *A Long Way from Home: Growing Up in the American Heartland in the Forties and Fifties* I was surprised to learn that there, too, the children carried lunch in Karo Syrup pails.

The school still had a bell in its tower. A long rope in the Boys' Hall ran up the length of the tower to the bell. Again, it was the older boys' task to ring it at appropriate times. I once tried to ring it, but

Interior of our one-room school. Note the Roman numeral clock in front of the classroom. This photo was taken three years before I attended.

did not have the strength to get a peep out of it. I loved the sound of that bell. But one day, near the end of my first year at school, all the students had to stand outside, a good distance away from the building. As we watched, the bell was dislodged, tumbling over the roof to the ground, sounding its own death knell as it fell.

The outhouses stood some distance behind the school building: one for the girls, and one for the boys. Since we were not allowed to enter each other's outhouses, I was curious what the boys' looked like inside. One day, when I was in second grade, after an older student rang the noon-hour bell (now a brass hand bell) I hung back behind the others to take a look inside the boy's outhouse. It looked just like the girls'; two big seats and one little seat. I didn't think anyone saw me. The next day, when I threatened to tattle on the seventh and eighth graders for smoking down by the river, Rita, a seventh grader, made it clear that if I was going to tattle on them, she would tell the teacher that I had looked into the boys' outhouse. That is how I learned what snitching and blackmail were.

The teacher we had in my first year of school left before the year was over. The neighborhood tavern keeper became the substitute teacher, qualified by a high school education. From second grade onward, we had Mrs. Bertha Schram, a woman in her forties with a college degree, whom I loved. I don't know how she did it, but she taught all eight grades totaling forty-five students. (There was no kindergarten.) In fact, it was from her that I received my first box of Prang watercolors during her monthly celebrations of her students' birthdays. She used her own money for this. Usually school supplies were purchased in bulk and one never knew the source. I copied down the brand name of Prang, and when I had used up the colors the teacher gave me, I found them in the dime store and bought a new set for myself.

After school let out, there were no books to read. One summer, the bookmobile came to our country school and we walked to meet it. The librarian called us "Honey" which made us laugh all the way home. It seemed so artificial. The limit was two books per student, but because I took good care of my books and never lost or damaged one, I was allowed to withdraw *three* books. Lucky me! I read all three books that same afternoon, and re-read them until the bookmobile came again three weeks later.

On the last day of school before Christmas vacation, around noon, we listened eagerly for the sound of sleigh bells that heralded the arrival of Santa. A neighbor had lent his horses and sleigh. Santa gave each child a brown bag of candy, nuts, and oh, a popcorn ball wrapped in colored cellophane! Then he distributed the gifts we had exchanged with other students. One year, I received *two* gifts. One of them was a Mickey Mouse pin that I cherished for years. When the eighth grade girls prepared the slips of paper for the exchange, they had accidentally put my name in twice. How could I have been so lucky? When I told my mother, she told me to ask the teacher if I should return one of the gifts, but happily, the teacher said I could keep both.

The large playground behind the school was surrounded by a double row of jack pines planted by the Civil Conservation Corps during the Great Depression. We had fun playing in and around them. Sometimes the girls played house in front of the school in the old lilac bushes. These were much taller than we were, and grew in clumps where previous generations had worn out paths among them.

Once I swung from the branch of a small tree that hung over the ditch on the edge of the playground. The branch broke. I was terrified because I had damaged school property. Should I tell the teacher what I had done? No one had seen me. Finally I decided that like George Washington and the cherry tree, I would tell the truth. I waited patiently at the teacher's desk until she looked up. I confessed. The teacher waved me away impatiently and said, "Don't bother me with such things." My noble gesture was all for naught!

In spring, the ditch ran with water replete with frog's eggs. It was exciting to seine them with a cloth and put them in a gallon jar, which we placed in the science corner. We watched them develop into tadpoles, then let them free in the river.

Once a week, during noon hour, "Old Lady Blair," as she was called, invited any four children to play bingo at her tiny two-room house just across the fence from the playground. She gave us lollipops and little prizes. It was such fun! In her tiny yard, she raised chickens. One of the big boys threw stones at the chickens from the playground side of the fence and killed one, and in so doing, he also killed our opportunity to play bingo and lick lollipops.

The big boys often beat up the younger girls on the way home from school. They pounded on our backs, threw our caps in the ditch, and hurled snowballs at us. Sometimes they washed our faces with snow or put it down our backs. The girls did their best to retaliate. It came to the point where the teacher held the big boys back to let the girls get a head start. It seemed some children had complained to their parents, who in turn complained to the school board. I was surprised because I thought we did a pretty good job fighting our own battles.

In third grade, I received a prize in a fire poster contest. Not much was made of this at home. During this year our district got a school bus. A girl on the bus shouted at me, "Catlicker, catlicker!" I flung back, "Doglicker, doglicker!" and that was the end of that. "Catlicker" was a derogatory term for a Catholic, and while my retort made no sense, I would not be victimized.

My mother taught me to have compassion for newcomers at school. So every year, I took the new girl under my wing, showed her around, and made friends with her. One year I got tired of being nice. I wondered what it would be like to be mean for a change. When a new girl named Natalie arrived, even though I liked her, by sheer force of will I went up to her, pulled her blond hair and told her she was ugly. I could see the hurt in her brown eyes. Shortly thereafter, I told her I didn't mean what I had said and asked her to play with me. We became good friends.

In fourth grade, I diagnosed myself with measles in the mirror above the sink in the boy's hall. With the teacher's permission, I walked home in blinding sunlight at high noon, right after a fresh snowfall. Since neither the school nor home had a phone, that was all I could do. I became nearsighted to the point where I could not read the big "E" on the eye chart. During eye screening, however, I always confidently said "E" and felt a little guilty about lying. Although I had the next two lines memorized, I did not say them, to prevent a false evaluation.

I had contracted the second strain of measles (rubeola), the first being the short or German version (rubella) which all of us had earlier. While my mother took good care of us when we were sick, she also had an instinct for knowing when we were getting well and had started to pretend, in order to receive more attention and get out of responsibilities.

By this time, I had read every book on my level the little library at the back of the schoolroom could offer. I began reading books above my level, one being *The Long Winter* by Laura Ingalls Wilder. I felt lucky to be living in a home that had more conveniences than the ones she described, and luckier still that I did not have to fight prairie fires!

Next, I started in on the encyclopedias. I didn't get very far because at the end of the year, when I was in fourth grade, the school closed and we went to the city school. My beloved school sold for one dollar and was converted to a car repair shop. I saw this as a desecration since to my mind, the school was a hallowed building. I wanted to live in that school.

After the schools consolidated, we attended Schofield Grade School. Oh, how many books there were! While *The Wizard of Oz* and *Alice in Wonderland* didn't interest me, I read the complete volumes of Andersen's and the Grimm brothers' fairy tales. I also devoured the Walter Farley books, the Nancy Drew series, and the remainder of the Laura Ingalls Wilder books.

When first attending the city school, the boys called my oldest sibling "Big boneyard," and the younger "Little boneyard." Despite eating well, we were as thin as beanpoles. My grandmother, who lived with us, often implied that we weren't being fed enough as she gently squeezed our upper arms. That really annoyed my mother, since although we were cash poor, we had more than enough to eat. Think fresh strawberries with real cream, pork, beef, and eggs from our own animals. It's just that we ran around so much; "Like wild animals," as Pavarotti said when he spoke of his childhood.

Initially, the city kids called me a dumb farmer. I didn't say anything. When my grades superseded those of my city counterparts, they stopped teasing. Now in fifth grade, I won a poppy poster contest. This seemed a big deal to me because now I had successfully competed with students at the city school.

Now I could not read the blackboard even if I sat in the front row. But I couldn't bring myself to tell the teacher that I couldn't see and instead accepted low grades on work done from the board. Every night I prayed for glasses, but was afraid to ask for them because they would be expensive. In catechism class, I learned that if you prayed hard enough for something, and if God thought it was good for you, you would get it. I decided to say fifty "Hail Marys" every night until I reached a thousand.

The county nurses screened the eyesight of the school children every year. On the first day of school the following year, the school nurse checked the students' eyes and said I needed glasses. I said they were too expensive and that my parents couldn't afford them. Then I missed the next two weeks of school to pick potatoes. One day during that time, the school nurse parked her car along side the field and asked the nearest person for my mother. My family was amused to

My second grade, fourth grade, and fifth grade photos.

see her trudging straight across the dusty field in her oxford shoes and nice navy blue dress with a white collar to talk to her. She spoke to my mother about something. At quitting time, my mother told me that the nurse said I needed glasses. To my surprise, my mother promptly made an appointment after potato season and I got a new pair of glasses! Neither of my parents gave me a hard time about the cost. I cannot say how grateful I was to that county nurse.

The next time I asked God for something was when I was eleven. In the Montgomery Ward catalog in the outhouse, I found a page with art supplies. I wanted the box of oil paints in tubes that came as a set with two brushes. In 1953 it cost $32, which was an outrageous amount, especially for something that was not a necessity. I cut out the sepia-toned product photograph and put it under my bed. It would be safe there since I was the one who cleaned the bedroom. Every night I knelt by my bed and prayed fifty "Hail Marys" for that box of paints. This time I upped the ante and promised three thousand "Hail Marys" in all.

Every morning when I looked under my bed there was only the picture of the box of paints. I never did complete three thousand prayers and eventually forgot about it. Years later, when I was 47, I signed up for an oil painting workshop in Minneapolis offered by Daniel Greene of New York. I ordered the customized box of paints listed for the program. When the parcel arrived, and I opened it, a faint memory stirred. I felt a frisson of recognition. There were the tubes of paint and two brushes pictured in the catalog I had prayed for 36 years ago! As an adult, I answered my own prayers once offered in childhood.

There were things advocated by adults that I questioned: I had my tonsils and adenoids removed at thirteen, then a four day hospital stay. Why did the nurses remove plants from my hospital room at night? (I had learned in science class that plants produced oxygen at night.) Why did they say "don't touch an electrical cord with wet hands?" (As long as you didn't let the moisture leak onto the prongs while inserting the cord, it was safe.) My mother said not to stare at the sun or I would become blind. (I stared at it. I did not become blind.) I was told that if I touched an electric wire I would be electrocuted. I climbed the fence to the pig house behind the toolshed and reached out to touch the wires that led to it, and nothing happened. (They were insulated, of course). My mother warned us of poison ivy. I went out and deliberately touched it and was not affected. Later I read that it had to be wet, or the leaves had to be crushed to release the resin.

Sometimes when I came home too excited about something I had learned at school, my mother, in the style of Larry David's grandfather in *Curb Your Enthusiasm,* put the lid on with "If you know so much, keep it to yourself." No point in getting a big head. As harmful as that attitude may seem, it did not quench my thirst for learning.

One summer day I thought I would test my mother to see how long she could keep finding work for me. So instead of disappearing as fast as I could after morning chores, I sat down on a chair in the kitchen and did nothing. I didn't even read. Soon I received a task. After completing it, I received another. This continued all day until 5 p.m., when my mother said, "Well, I guess you can go now." I never told her what I had been up to. I had proven the point to myself, that I wasn't just imagining it: as long as I was in sight I'd get another chore.

I had four daily chores: dress my little sister, carry wood, carry water, and gather eggs. When my mother told me to set the table, I'd set it and then sit down to read until she told me to add this or that to the setting. I would comply and then return to the book. In exasperation, she would say "Every time I want you to do something, you have your nose in a book." It was true.

My parents were usually more concerned about the behavior

section of the report card than the grades. They always supported the teachers if there was a behavior problem, which was seldom. If either parent learned from a tattletale sibling that one of us did something wrong in school, we were scolded again at home. If we were not guilty, my mother said we deserved the scolding nevertheless for the times we got away with something without getting caught.

In seventh grade, when attending D.C. Everest High, the bus ride was an hour and a half each way. I got home at five in the evening. My teacher, Mr. B, indicated on my report card that I didn't read enough, obviously confusing me with some other student. When my mother read that, her expression was priceless. For the first and only time in my life, she stood up for me against a teacher and wrote, "I disagree with '1b' for voluntary reading. All her spare time is spent reading books." ("1b" meant 'very good but is capable of much more and better work'.) I felt vindicated. It was like math; two negatives made a positive. Not

to be outdone, on the next report Mr. B wrote, "Has showed improvement in voluntary reading by giving very good reports in class. She could improve her penmanship."

It was at this school, in industrial arts class, that I developed a crush on Darrell. We chased each other around the worktables. I liked him because he was intelligent, had integrity, and looked me in the eye. But I knew it could never fly because he was not Catholic.

The city girls liked me, and my classmates elected me cheerleader. I was so excited to be accepted by them, plus I could legitimately "show off" in front of the student body. I so much

Back page of my report card showing exchange between my mother and the teacher.

wanted to be part of what the other girls did. Of course, I couldn't, because school was five miles away and I had no way to get home after practice or a game. Once I asked my mother why Dad wouldn't take us to school activities. She explained that he was tired of driving because he drove the tractor back and forth over the same rows in the fields for cultivating, harrowing, seeding, weeding and harvesting. I could only imagine how boring that was. Still, I envied my classmates.

I was thirteen the first time I used a telephone. During the one year I attended a parochial school, St. Therese Grade School, a friend asked me to call her mother. I didn't know what to say and blurted something or other, annoying her mother. The girl got a kick out of that, but I was mortified. That year, the first grade teacher asked my teacher if one of her students could pull vocabulary flashcards for her students. She would pay fifty cents. I felt honored to be chosen and even to be paid, so every morning I conscientiously performed the task before classes began. Once my teacher asked me to monitor the class for half an hour when she had to leave. These assignments gave me a sense of confidence.

The schools kept consolidating, and I ended up attending four different elementary schools. At first, our old friends came along with us; later, we were thrust into a school with all unknown students. Without realizing it, I was developing PR skills.

Potatoes were the cash crop on our farm, which means they were produced for the market rather than for our personal use. Since the potato harvest season lasted about three weeks, and we grew twenty acres of the tubers, it extended into the beginning of the school year in September. Our county had no "potato vacation" as our neighboring county did, so we always missed the first week or two of school.

At the age of six, I had to pick only four hours a day before the school year started. I felt lucky and yet guilty that my older sisters had to miss school. At the age of seven, my workday extended to an eight-hour day (with an hour off at noon) during those weeks before school started. By third grade, I too, was old enough to pick potatoes and miss school until the season finished. I was so sorry to miss school.

When I complained, my mother put it in perspective by saying she had to pick rocks when she was a girl. She grew up about thirty miles away where the glacier stopped and left its accumulation of rocks and rich, dark soil. Our farm had sandy soil, the rich soil having been scraped off by the glacier.

We were allowed to attend the first day of school to orient ourselves, get a desk, and tell the teacher we would be out for the next two weeks. The teachers rolled their eyes and groaned. Some became angry. Twelve years later, when I became a schoolteacher, I understood. When we returned to school we had to play "catch up." I always made a friend the first day of school to be sure I had a friend when I returned.

The hard part of picking potatoes was that each of us had a portion of a row to pick after the tractor pulled the potato digger through. The objective was to pick it before the machinery made a complete round so that the wide tractor tire, which extended beyond the row, wouldn't destroy the potatoes dug up from the previous round. Besides, if we picked fast enough, we got a rest, or could pick wild cherries at the edge of the field, until the tractor came around again.

Also, at the far end of the field a gallon of water in a tin Karo Syrup pail provided refreshment. Being the youngest, I never got my portion picked fast enough. The tractor always seemed to be at my heels so I never got a rest. Sometimes my mother or older cousin came to help me. I often held up the operation and was thereby considered not a good worker.

We wore straw hats to ward off sunstroke. It was fun getting a brand new straw hat every summer, sometimes with flowers stenciled on it. We also got new, clean, brown cotton work gloves. The gloves became muddy and the fingertips wore through before the season was over, at which point they had to be replaced.

I was glad to be Catholic, because it meant it was a sin to work on Sunday. At least we didn't have to do dishes during potato picking season. Grandma did them for us. Saturday housecleaning went by the wayside, too. In school, we learned that child labor was against the law. Armed with that information, we confronted our parents, only to learn that it was legal for children to work on a family farm. I felt the government had betrayed me.

A hundred-pound bag of potatoes sold for about $1.89, less if sold wholesale to a potato chip company. One night, early in the season, my father came home from town with an order from a merchant for $4.00 a hundredweight if he could get them to him by 8:00 the next morning. We were so excited! We rose at 4:00 a.m. and were picking by 4:30. Dad had to use the tractor lights to see the rows. After picking, the potatoes had to be sorted to eliminate any with defects such as scabs or rot. We met the deadline and it was a good thing, because by noon, the price had dropped by a dollar, and by the next day it had leveled off to its usual price.

Although we never received an allowance, our parents paid us two dollars for a full day's work, and employed my cousins for four dollars a day. I asked my mother why that was, since it didn't seem fair. She replied, "You live here." Some farmers' kids thought we were lucky to be paid at all.

My mother opened a bank account for each of us and every fall we deposited our earnings into a savings account. Gifts of money also were deposited. We received a little brown bankbook with cream-colored pages just like our parents'. In it was typed "minor," with the date and amount of deposit stamped in respective columns. From our earnings, we put fifty cents into a little envelope every Sunday to put into the collection basket. It was a difficult thing to do, partly because it was hard earned, and partly because for a young child to endure the Mass and sermon was difficult in itself.

At the end of the potato season, my father obtained a permit to burn the dried brown potato vines. This was done at night when the wind had died down. The vines were gathered into a stack and set ablaze with sparks flying and flames shooting high into the air, or so it seemed. So beautiful in the night! We ran around barefoot in the soft soil as the flames cast shadows of furrow upon furrow, each becoming smaller as it receded into the distance.

In July, we picked beans all day. We had to pick fast, yet without pulling up the bean bush by the roots in the process. The canning companies paid nine cents a pound for the small beans and two or three cents a pound for the larger ones. Although it was much easier to fill a large mesh bag with the large beans, the drop in profit offset the satisfaction. I always tried to pick eighty pounds of the larger beans, which took me a whole day to fill one bag.

Once, to make extra money, I picked for the neighbors. After picking for only an hour, Grace, the lovely elderly neighbor woman, asked me to come in for a break and have cookies. "No, that's okay," I said. Later she invited me again, but it was against my training to loll about having cookies when I had promised to work. We did not take breaks. So schooled was I in the work ethic that at times in my life, I have refused pleasant opportunities because I did not want to be too easy on myself.

We never wasted water, not because it wasn't plentiful, but because every drop we used we pumped by hand. I think sometimes prosperity breeds waste. There was a small hand pump for water inside the house and a large one outside for washing vegetables and keeping water in the cows' drinking tank. Speaking of the water tank, sometimes to entertain our city cousins, we threw a chicken or cat into it to see how quickly it flew out. My dad kept bullheads in it in summer since they were bottom feeders and helped keep the tank clean. Over winter they lived in a water barrel in the barn.

One of our chores was to pump the water for the drinking pail in the kitchen and the reservoir in the stove. The night before washday, we pumped water into a large, oblong copper double boiler to be heated and poured into the washing machine by the bucketful. When canning season began, the boiler was used to heat water for sterilizing and sealing jars.

In July, my mother drove Grandpa's Model A Ford to go berry picking in the brush near a woods. Since the property was sometimes posted, my mother always asked permission of the landowner. We picked quarts and quarts of raspberries, blackberries, and black raspberries, according to season. This provided us with canned fruit and jam for the winter. We tied a cloth belt around our waists with an empty Karo Syrup bucket attached in front, leaving both hands free for picking. At age six, I wasn't very good at it. Usually mine turned to mush as I trounced around, causing the red juice of the raspberries to turn purple and blue as the acid interacted with the tin pail. The bees accompanied us as we performed the hot prickly task for hours on end. The greatest number of berry bushes attracted the largest number of bees.

Always ready to help, Grandma went with us. At noon, we found a clearing in the woods, sat under a grove of birch trees and eagerly ate the cucumber sandwiches my mother had packed along with homemade lemonade. Because of the heat, she buttered the bread instead of using salad dressing. Those picnic lunches were as idyllic and pastoral as anyone could imagine, with birds singing and wildflowers all about. Afterward we picked some more berries until it was time to go home and prepare supper. Sometimes I wasn't taken along because I wasn't as productive as my older sisters. I was relieved to have avoided the work, but also disappointed that I was being left out.

Canning was a lot of work in the hottest part of summer when all the produce ripened at the same time. Earlier in the season, we hulled quarts and quarts of strawberries, which my mother made into jam. Since air in the jar promotes bacterial growth, my mother skimmed off and let us eat the pink foam from the jam cooking in a huge, white-flecked, blue enamel pot. We knew just when to hang around the kitchen for that foam and when to scoot, when we sensed there was work looming. My mother even canned beef and chicken, making sure that they were cooked and sealed properly to avoid botulism.

Everything was preserved since we had to be self-sufficient during the winter. There were only a few trips to town, ten miles away, for sugar and flour, which we purchased in fifty-pound bags—in Laura Ingalls Wilder style. Usually my mother also bought grapefruit and oranges, cough medicine, and sewing materials.

Despite the hot weather in late July, we wore long sleeved shirts to protect our arms from the stubble of the sheaves as we shocked oats to prepare it for threshing. Often the scratchy straw pricked through the fabric and the field stubble poked at our ankles. At the end of the day, we rubbed our arms with Corn Huskers Lotion, a soothing gel that was mostly glycerin. It worked like magic.

On the far left, I'm glad because I got out of berry picking. Grandpa's Model A Ford is parked behind the gate.

A harvester cut and bundled the ripened oats with twine before we set it up in shocks. We spread the bottom of each bundle for "feet" and set up eight of them. We started with leaning two "heads" against each other in the center, two more opposite them, then four more thrust around those with the ninth one lying on top to act as an umbrella to protect the center from rain. There was usually a week of that. We did the same with the one or two acres of rye we'd planted. If the oats got soaked before the threshing, it would spoil from mold or rot; but rye would smell like beer.

After the oats were done, we ran around in the evening playing hide-and-seek behind the shocks until it got dark. Before threshing, we kicked the shocks apart so they would dry from the inside. Sometimes there was a nest of pink baby mice inside. We were instructed to stamp the life out of them since they were future grain usurpers. It was a hard thing to do, and sometimes I didn't.

Threshing day was most exciting. The loud diesel tractor pulling the dinosaur-like threshing machine around the house woke us up. We jumped out of bed so as not to miss the excitement. After morning chores, we went to watch, with strict orders to go no closer than the clothes line posts, because the machinery was dangerous. The threshing machine was powered by a long belt connected to the diesel tractor. The sound was deafening. We sat under the clothes line to watch the men use pitchforks to feed bundles of oats into the jaws of the monster.

The machine deposited the winnowed grain into bags and blew the chaff into the barn. All the neighbors worked for each other's harvests, thereby eliminating the need for wages. The older men did the lighter work, the younger, the more strenuous. Only the thresher charged for the use of his machine. The young men hoisted the sacks of grain up on their backs to carry them to the granary. There they emptied them into a huge bin on the first floor where the auger pulled it up to the second floor. As we three sisters watched, we opined which young men were most handsome. Usually one who wore no shirt.

We watched until we were called in to help prepare the substantial dinner at noon. No one referred to it as "lunch." At church the previous Sunday, the women consulted each other to ensure each served a different menu. All the extra leaves were inserted into the table, which was then covered with a white linen tablecloth and set for about twenty men. Before entering the house, the men washed their faces and arms under the outdoor pump. Years later, I was surprised to see this in a painting by Grant Wood, *Dinner for Threshers*. I liked to connect my experience with the rest of the world, because I felt we were isolated.

After the meal, the men, who were always polite and appreciative, rested briefly and then returned to work until evening. Meanwhile, grandma helped us with the clean up. Sometimes in mid-afternoon, when it was a particularly hot day, my mother sent us out to the field with lemonade for the men pitching the bundles of oats onto the hay wagon. When the threshing machine stopped, the silence was palpable. The food served for supper differed from the previous meal. The tired men always praised my mother's cooking, especially the lemon meringue pie. I later read that they would sometimes drag out their work day a little so they could get two meals at the same place if the cook was a good one. I guess that explains why they always stayed for two meals at our house.

The day after threshing, we ran to the straw stack to scavenge pieces of binder twine where the masterful threshing jaws had cut them from the sheaves of oats. We tied them together to form lengths to braid, and "Presto!" we had jump ropes.

All summer long, we ran to the straw stack in the barn to get drinking straws. We peeled off the outer sleeve to reveal the inner straw that was impeccably clean. Sometimes we used these straws to drink homemade root beer, which my mother made from Hires extract; it was a perfect thing to do on a hot day. I always tried to find a thin straw to make the drink last longer. I liked to sit on the back porch and hear the hot summer breeze sing through the screen, which it struck at just the right angle to produce a whistling sound; the sound of summer.

When I turned six, we walked a mile to church to attend catechism class on Saturdays because we were public school students. I memorized the Baltimore Catechism No. 1 from cover to blue cover:

"Who made you?" "God made me."

"Who is God?" "God is the Supreme Being who made all things."

I could relate to that since I picked beans every summer and sometimes there was a really big one. I imagined God as a sort of Jolly Green Giant.

At catechism I learned about Adam and Eve and original sin. It had nothing to do with my actions; I, like everyone else, was automatically born with it. I felt hopeless and depressed at this unfair indictment. What was the point of being good if I was guilty of a sin I did not commit? I learned that while this stain was removed at Baptism, everyone would always be inclined to sin. I was mad at Adam and Eve for creating this problem.

At age six I was old enough to go to school, old enough to work, and old enough to sin. I loved being old enough to do the first, hated the second, and thought I committed many of the third. I learned that at that age I was considered morally responsible for my actions. The Catholic Church considered it the age of reason. At five, I heard from

Grant Wood's *Dinner for Threshers.*

my older sisters that one could not commit a sin until one reached the age of reason at six. I tried to commit as many sins as I could before I turned six, reasoning that they would not count, since I had not yet reached the age of reason. The problem was, I did not make my first confession and communion until I was nine, so between the ages of six and nine, I feared that I might die and go to hell. Then I learned that if I said the Act of Contrition and was truly sorry, I would be forgiven even before I made my first confession. Scrupulous, I considered myself a regular sinner, so the Act of Contrition crossed my lips many times during the day, in case there was an accident. Later, I learned that technically, the age of reason was seven. Darn!

For my first holy communion we had a big celebration, inviting my baptismal sponsors and both sets of Grandparents. I felt lucky to have known both in my lifetime.

I learned about sin from the Saturday morning catechism classes. We did not believe that we could commit a sin, go to confession, and cavalierly commit it again as some non-Catholics thought. No. We were taught that to be forgiven, we had to make an honest effort not to commit that sin again. The priest in the confessional then assigned a penance, which was a number of Our Father's and Hail Mary's, the number depending on the number and seriousness of sins.

We studied the many categories of actual sin: mortal sin, venial sin, sins of omission and sacrilege. There were the Ten Commandments, Six Laws of the Church, Four Cardinal sins, the Seven Deadly sins, and others too numerous to mention. Every night I examined my conscience and said the act of contrition in case I would die during the night.

(left) On my first communion day with my parents. (above) With my paternal grandparents, Stasia and John, on the left, and my maternal grandparents, Leo and Helen, on the right.

In preparation for weekly confession, I scrupulously pored over all the sins I could possibly commit, anxious to include all that applied to me. One of the sins listed was "performing one's marital duties." Since I didn't know what "marital" meant, I assumed it referred to chores. When I confessed it, the priest in the confessional asked, "How old are you?"

I attribute my highly developed analytical skills to applying the Baltimore Catechism criteria for mortal sin to my actions. I mentally argued each point, trying to figure out a way that I had not met one of the conditions.

It was also a sin to doubt one's faith, but by the time I was nine years old, I had doubts about the existence of God. I reasoned that so many people of limited means contributed to the church to make kids behave. To test the existence of God, I took my little calendar with a picture of the Sacred Heart of Jesus off my bedroom wall and propped it up on the storage chest. On this clear cloudless day, I told myself I would spit on that picture, and if there was a God, he would strike me dead with a bolt of lightning. I spat. Held my breath. Nothing happened. That proved God did not exist.

Not one to be impressed with movie stars or pop singers, I admired people who invented things or achieved heroic feats. I liked to read the lives of the saints because of the gory stories of those who were martyrs. In a way, I thought they were lucky, because after a

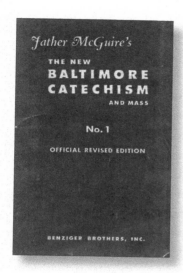

35. **What is mortal sin?**
    Mortal sin is a grievous offense against the law of God.

36. **Why is this sin called mortal?**
    This sin is called mortal because it takes away the life of the soul.

37. **What three things are necessary to make a sin mortal?**
    To make a sin mortal these three things are necessary: first, the thought, desire, word, action, or omission must be seriously wrong or considered seriously wrong;
    second, the sinner must know it is seriously wrong;
    third, the sinner must fully consent to it.

38. **What is venial sin?**
    Venial sin is a less serious offense against the law of God.

(left) I memorized all the answers to 212 questions in *The New Baltimore Catechism No. 1.* (above) I pored over the three criteria necessary for a mortal sin listed in number 37.

short time of suffering they went straight to heaven and no longer had to work, say prayers or follow rules.

Once a year, despite my father's protests, my mother took each of us by Greyhound bus to the dentist in town, ten miles away. I looked forward to this trip even though to save money, we often had our teeth drilled without Novocaine—"unless you really can't stand it," my mother allowed. That was when I vowed never to eat candy again—a vow I never kept. The best part of all was having my mother all to myself that day. After seeing the dentist, she took me to the lunch counter in the basement of Woolworth's and we each ordered an ice cream soda. I could choose any flavor I wanted. When they arrived, we sat there together enjoying the pleasure of the moment.

Visiting the dentist meant I not only went to the city of Wausau, which was exciting in itself, but I got to spend a dime any way I liked. My mother patiently took me from Woolworth's to McClellan's to Ben Franklin's dime stores and back again, shopping for the best possible book of paper dolls. On one of those trips, when I was ten, a gentleman customer and I were at the counter at the same time, I having been there first. When the clerk chose to wait on him first, he informed her that I had been there before him. I will not forget how special it made me feel that an adult deferred to me.

Another favorite destination was Jahnke Book Store, which also sold religious goods. With my bean-picking money I once bought a little plastic figurine of the Blessed Virgin Mary—one that glowed in the dark.

My mother often took pictures of her children with her Brownie camera. She also took pictures of relatives when they came to visit and when we visited them. Sometimes you could recognize the same dress on a different sibling in the following year's photo.

Cats were my favorite farm animal, and I always made one my pet. I was teased about my affection for cats. Sometimes I got a wet washcloth from the house and cleaned out the dust from their ears. They didn't seem to mind. One day, I decided a cat's whiskers were too long. I engaged the assistance of a sibling who held down the cat while I snipped its whiskers down to stubble. The cat disappeared forever.

We knew that people dropped off cats on our country road because every so often a new one would suddenly appear. One cold morning in late fall, a white Angora cat lay barely visible in the large gap beneath the tool shed door. When we approached, It did not move. It was frozen solid. We knew immediately it was a city cat,

Here we are, before my youngest sister was born. I'm second from right.

Now including my little sister, but with another sibling missing. I'm mugging for the camera because I'm thinking family poses are too boring.

because it didn't know enough to find its way to the barn. If a cat died in summer, we buried it in a shoe box in front of the barn. We sowed oats over it because it sprouted rapidly, looking like the grass on the cemetery lawn.

Admiring a neighbor's riding horse while holding my younger sister's hand.

I also made a pet of a baby chick, which I named "Dusty." I wanted the challenge of taming an animal that was naturally timid. That endeavor proved disastrous. Each mother hen had her own little coop with her chicks. The grate opened just enough for the chicks to get out and run around. In the evening, after the chicks all went back to their respective mothers and coops, my mother shut the grate for the night to keep out the varmints. When it was getting its second feathers, my emboldened pet chick went into the wrong coop. Since the mother hen did not recognize it as her own, she pecked it to death, nearly decapitating it. I cried and cried in secret. Then I put it into my best white box—from a first communion gift—and wrapped it round and round with lavender string from a rug-making bobbin. I did not bury it but hid it behind a spool of barbed wire leaning against the back of the barn. When I went to check on it the next spring, the box was gone.

Petting a rooster with one hand, while holding it securely by the feet with the other.

Since Thanksgiving wasn't a Holy day of the Church, we didn't celebrate it. Because there was no school that day, it was a perfect opportunity to haul wood. We slid it down the handmade metal chute through the basement window, then neatly stacked it against the wall.

On the day before Christmas, my father took us to "the back forty" to cut down a Christmas tree. It had to be fresh because we lit real candles on it on Christmas Eve, since we did not have electricity. If there was a big empty space in the tree, my father drilled a hole into the trunk and inserted an extra branch taken from the bottom. The tree stand was the curved side of a half log, in which he drilled a large hole to hold the trunk. We did not buy anything we could make ourselves.

That afternoon, once we'd selected a tree and brought it home, we decorated it with ornaments including three tagboard paper sculptures: a gold paper airplane and a soldier and sailor with 3-D folds that puffed out their chests. My mother called them World War II ornaments because she bought them during that time when there was a shortage of other materials. There were also spray-painted bird ornaments made of one of the first plastics developed. My mother hung marshmallows amid the other ornaments. A red cellophane garland festooned the tree.

How did Santa know what to bring? Every November we received mail order toy catalogs. My mother told us to look through the catalog to find a toy we wanted, with the restriction that Santa could only afford presents up to $8.00. It was fun to pick whatever we wanted, then to narrow it down to what we wanted most.

Once, when I was six, I sassed my mother back. She had warned me to stop it or Santa wouldn't bring me anything, to which I had petulantly replied, "I don't care! I don't care if Santa doesn't bring me anything!" But he did bring me something: stones and two sticks. Did it scar me for life? I don't know, because I still love Christmas. Did it improve my behavior? I don't know about that either.

I tried to believe in Santa as long as possible, because it meant that I would receive two presents; one from Santa in my stocking and one from my parents under the Christmas tree. When I reached fifth grade I tried to convince my mother that I still believed in Santa, though I had long since learned the truth. She said, "Don't you think you're getting to be a little too old to believe in Santa?"

When I was ten, we each received three gifts from our parents on Christmas. One of mine was *Eight Cousins* by Louisa May Alcott. A book of my own! I was deeply touched and surprised that my mother realized how much that would mean to me.

On Christmas Eve we brought down gifts for one another and placed them under the tree, and hung our long stockings on the clothesline behind the stove. Just before supper, in Polish custom, we wished each other a "Merry Christmas" as we exchanged pieces of opłatki (pronounced "opwatki"). These were wafers embossed with nativity scenes, blessed at church the Sunday before. As we exchanged pieces with our siblings, we also had to say we were sorry for anything we had done that year to hurt them, a phrase that was nearly impossible to get out of our mouths after we'd been quarreling with them all year!

After supper, we went to the basement to watch my father open the little door at the side of the coal furnace "so Santa could come out when he came down the chimney." I couldn't understand how a big fat Santa could squeeze through that little door, but I finally decided he could manage because he was really a spirit.

In the middle of the night, we were awakened to attend Midnight Mass at the mission church a mile away, during which we three oldest girls sang in the choir. The next morning, down the steep stairs we tumbled, to see what Santa had put in our stockings. Every year, a few new ornaments appeared on the tree.

Then off to Church again for 8:00 a.m. Christmas Day Mass. After a special meal, everyone gathered around the tree. The youngest able to read distributed the gifts, which were then opened by each recipient according to age; oldest first, the youngest deferring gratification until all the others had shown their gifts. Grandma Wanta always gave us socks for which we dutifully expressed our thanks with as much enthusiasm as we could muster. Sometimes I shut the pocket doors of the living room and contemplated the beauty of the tree in silence, wishing this day would never end.

Christmas night was especially enchanting when we lit candles on the tree and sang "Kolędy" (pronounced "Kolendy"). This is a collection of Polish Christmas carols that includes a favorite lullaby, "Lulajże, Jezuniu." My grandparents enjoyed joining us. The candles burned on the outermost branches of the freshly cut tree, and a bucket of water stood nearby just in case. On the Sunday after Christmas, we took down the tree and had fun roasting the remaining marshmallows over a candle or the dying embers in the stove.

My mother salvaged the candle stubs, warmed them in a pie tin and pressed them with her fingers to form a large flat piece. From this she cut shapes of stars, bells, and trees using Christmas cookie cutters. Then she threaded them and let them cool. The next year when they were hung on the tree, the light shone through them, resembling stained glass.

Weddings lasted three days. The day before the wedding a special dinner was served at the house of the bride. Silverware and paper

napkins stood upright in tall glasses at intervals along the center of the row of tables covered with white cloths. Relatives prepared and contributed food. Chickens were butchered and plucked in advance. There was a variety of wonderful homemade pies for dessert.

An ornament my mother made from candle stubs.

The next morning, the wedding was held in church, followed by a huge breakfast at a local dance hall. That, in turn, was followed by dancing in the afternoon and evening. A band was hired to play polkas and waltzes. We could have all the soda pop we wanted and would boast to one another how many bottles we had drunk. Near the end of the evening, every guest tossed a dollar into a cigar box before taking turns dancing with the bride. At the age of ten I didn't know how to dance but put in a fifty-cent piece my mother had given me and was thrilled to "dance" with the bride, Aunt Hattie, as I remember.

The following day, a mock wedding was held at the dance hall, during which the man dressed as a bride and the woman dressed as a groom. The "groom" carried a shotgun as a tease that it had been a "shotgun wedding." Then everyone sat down to eat the plentiful leftovers. Afterward, there was a "shivaree" where a group played on a saw and washboards, and clashed pot lids as cymbals while the guests danced.

When my city cousins visited, they thought farm work was fun, much to our chagrin. After visiting the animals, we liked to jump off the hayloft into the straw stack 14 feet below. They raved about my mother's homemade bread, although we preferred store-bought bread. Bought bread was smooth and didn't have holes in it which allowed syrup to leak through. The city cousins enjoyed eating fresh country chicken, while we country cousins liked the hot dogs served at their place. I liked the sidewalks in the city because they kept my shoes from getting dirty.

One Saturday, in anticipation of relatives visiting, my mother had heaped two pie crusts with sliced apples and then poured sugar over them, ready for the top crust. As I walked past them, I snitched a couple of slices with the most sugar on them. But mistakenly, my mother had used salt instead of sugar. Quickly I sneaked outside and spat out the slices, but didn't tell my mother about her mistake, because then she would have known I had my finger in the pie, so to speak. After the meal on Sunday, as the pie was served, I waited in anticipation hoping that somehow my mother had caught the error. Soon all the faces around the table took on a peculiar expression. Everyone was too polite to say anything. When my mother sat down and tasted it, she was so embarrassed I regretted I hadn't told her about the salt.

After these meals for up to seventeen people, there were mountains of dishes to do. Company was not allowed to help. Oh, how I hated doing the dishes while the men went out on the porch to smoke cigars. Once, after a lot of back and forth about how she was a guest and shouldn't be working, my Aunt Hattie insisted that we girls go out and play. She was the only aunt who had ever done that. We liked her, my mother's youngest sister, the best of all. She could sing brilliantly and could even yodel. She cared for us while my mother went to the hospital to have my youngest sister, and in turn, when we grew up, we helped care for her children when she had her babies.

Spankings were swift and effective, sometimes with a switch, sometimes with a strap. My mother said she was not going to hurt her hand spanking me. Hmmm. I had never thought about the spanker, only of the spankee. If it was winter and I intuited a spanking was in the offing, I quickly put on my thick, woolen snow pants, and after a reasonable number of spanks, I feigned crying so it would stop before it really hurt. Once, my mother told my father to spank me. He had a hard time with that and gave me three spanks I could hardly feel. I faked crying anyway. It was the best spanking I ever had. It was then that I learned my father was tenderhearted.

On one occasion, my mother gave me a short time out. I think she got the idea from one of my aunts. I sat in my parents' bedroom on a chair with the alarm clock placed on another chair facing me. My mother said when the little hand got to the three and the big hand on six, I could leave. I thought that was the cat's meow and couldn't believe I got away without a spanking. But it gave me time to think about what I had done, and that perhaps next time I might not be so lucky.

There were no such things as rummage sales. No one had anything superfluous. When someone brought us a box of outgrown toys or clothes, we could select what we wanted according to age. I always got third choice, and it shows on a snapshot where we three girls are holding dolls, I with the smallest. But on one occasion the third choice worked well for me. When we received a box of clothing that included hats, by default I got one I liked. This was just after World War II and the hat design had been influenced by the military. It resembled a soldier's garrison cap and gave me the prestigious feeling of a soldier.

When ballpoint pens were first invented, the interior cartridge could be replaced when the ink ran out. Magic markers could also be refilled with ink. Later, the whole pen was thrown away because replacement parts were no longer available. We thought it wasteful, not aware that we were in the process of becoming a throwaway society.

My mother curled our hair with "Toni" brand permanent wave, and to save on cost always bought two sets for us three girls. She used the left over lotions for me, the third girl. By the time my turn came it was late at night. I sat on mail order catalogs in the high chair so she could reach my head conveniently. I kept nodding off, throwing her off while she turned my hair in thin paper wrappers around the curlers.

We were self-sustaining in every way possible, not because it was eco-friendly, but because it was economical. Every year, my mother sewed each of us girls Easter dresses made of flour sacks. This was one time we did not wear a hand-me-down. For a whole year, my mother

Second from left, I am unhappy with the smallest doll, looking enviously at my oldest sister's big beautiful one.

saved flour sacks with designs printed on them. She instructed my father always to select two sacks with identical designs when he and my grandfather went to town. Three girls at the time meant six sacks of flour. Since my mother and grandmother baked everything from scratch—at least three loaves of bread a week plus rolls, cakes, and cookies—they used a lot of flour.

A typical sack of flour was white; the ones we bought had printed designs and an extra portion extending beyond its normal rectangular size, making it a yard square. Two yards were needed for one dress. We could pick out the style of dress we wanted by looking at the girls' dresses in the Sears & Roebuck and the Montgomery Ward catalogs. "Wishbooks," my mother called them. She adapted a basic pattern to almost any style we chose. When we wore them to church with our Easter hats, people praised my mother, who was justifiably proud of our appearance.

My dad owned a .22 for shooting the occasional skunk in the yard or muskrat in the basement, but mostly for butchering a pig every

Ready for church on Sunday morning. On the far right, I'm feeling smart in my third choice hat.

fall. He hated shooting the pig. He never even went deer hunting. Shooting the pig was rather poignant as it was fed corn, which it was never otherwise fed, to entice it into a corner where it became a better target. Dad shot it just above and between the eyes, so it would die without suffering.

My mother told me never to watch afterward when they bled it by slitting its throat. Once, I looked anyway and almost vomited. I can see the scene to this day. So once in a while it proved worthwhile to listen to my mother. We spent the rest of the day cleaning and butchering the pig. First, my father and grandfather hoisted it above a cauldron of boiling water in the fireplace of the toolshed, then dipped it in to scald it so they could scrape off the hair with a circular scraper. Then they disemboweled it, which was always interesting because I could see and identify the various inner organs.

My mother and grandmother scraped the small intestines and soaked them in lye until they were pink and clean, to be used as casings for the sausage. By the end of the day, we each had taken our turn grinding the meat by hand to fill those casings. I wanted very much to extract the eyeball of the pig as its head lay in a large aluminum pan. I wanted to dissect it to locate the parts of the eye I had studied in science class, but the muscles were so strong, I couldn't do it. That evening, we shared the sausage with neighbors. Since we had no telephone, arrangements had been made at the previous Sunday's Mass for them to come by and pick it up. No one talked about building community; we just did it.

All of this had to be done in one day in October when it was cool, since we had no refrigeration. While we worked, the men took the carcass to a freezer locker in Hatley, nine miles away, to be hung, chilled, cut up, and frozen. When the weather became cold enough, the slab pork was salted down and stored in a barrel in the toolshed. On Sunday mornings, it was convenient to run out to the shed before 8 o'clock Mass to take out a slab to thaw while we attended the service. Afterward my mother sliced it as bacon for a hearty breakfast.

As much as my father hated to shoot the pig, my mother hated to chop off the chicken's head. But someone had to do it. Often on a Sunday morning before going to church, my mother donned her farm clothes and did the deed. It was a quick death, though you wouldn't know it the way the chicken ran around without its head. The chicken roasted in the oven of the wood-burning stove while we worshiped. My mother selected hardwood, which burned slowly and evenly.

In winter, Jack Frost painted the windows with broad sweeps and swoops. It's been a long time since I've seen frost on windows. At night, my mother lit the kerosene lamp with its glass chimney and tole-painted base. I thrilled to the sound of the howling wicked winter wind. The house had been built at an angle so its corner would split the northwest wind.

Early on, we slept three to a bed, I in the middle with the blankets skimming over me while my two older sisters curled the ends around themselves. Although I never knew a good-night kiss, I felt one when my mother came upstairs on a cold winter night to spread an extra blanket on our beds. It felt good even if I wasn't cold.

For quilts, my mother saved old woolen skirts and sweaters and sent them to the woolen mills in Faribault, Minnesota. There, for a price, the wool was reprocessed and returned to us in the form of blankets and batting for quilts. Grandma helped my mother tie little yarn pieces at measured intervals to bind the batting to a cotton cover which was spread out on the floor upstairs.

A favorite family pleasure on Saturday nights in winter was to sit around the table, eat popcorn, and read; sometimes comic books, sometimes books from school. Dad read *Popular Mechanics* magazine and my mother *The Farmer's Wife* magazine. We grew our own popcorn, rubbing the dried cobs against each other to loosen the kernels. We each had a paper plate heaped high with popcorn accompanied by a glass of canned grapefruit juice. It was a perfect combination of texture and flavor. At Christmas, my mother made popcorn balls. The syrup recipe had molasses in it. It was so tasty, but I have never found it in store-bought popcorn balls.

My mother liked to try out new recipes. If we didn't like something on our plates, she would say, "Eat half of it." This seemed like a fair compromise. Sometimes, if I really didn't like something, I used the excuse that I had to use the outhouse, stuffed my mouth with the offending food, and spat it out behind the rose bush.

Despite the work, living on the farm had its own sensory rewards. There is nothing like the smell of newly turned earth in spring, and in summer the freshly mowed hay has its own perfume. We pulled the tiny petals from the red clover and sucked the honey from them. An early riser, I often took a walk before the family was up. I thrilled to the song of the meadowlark high up on the telegraph lines, inhaled the fragrant fresh air, and admired the morning light transforming the dew into prisms of shimmering colors on each blade of grass. All the more beautiful, these, because they were transient, I concluded. I have not heard a meadowlark since.

When a summer rainstorm approached in the evening, we rushed out with dessert in hand, to sit on the northwest side of the house to watch the dramatic thunderclouds break. Then heavy raindrops chased us back into the house. At night, the sound of rain on the roof was a lullaby that put me to sleep. Another pleasant way to fall asleep was to hear the sound of the Doppler effect of the steam locomotive in the night, the sound frequency of the whistle suddenly dropping as it passed.

If a severe thunderstorm came in the middle of the night, my mother awakened all of us to go downstairs so we would be together in case of danger. Sometimes, she lit a holy candle or burned blessed flowers in an old pie tin on the stove. As a result, I never feared or panicked during storms.

Every spring my mother and one or two of us girls would chase the cows from the barn to the cow pasture. My mother named the cows: Spotty, Redhead, Thunder, Lightning. Grandpa installed a solid white block of salt as a salt lick under the eaves of the cowshed where it was shielded from the rain. As the cows carved concave hollows with their coarse tongues, it gradually became a beautiful skeletal sculpture. By the end of summer, it had disappeared entirely. If a cow calved during the summer, my father put it in the front seat beside him in the panel truck and drove it home, drawing stares from strangers along the way. He tethered it near the barn for the summer where it would be safe.

Sometimes between guiding the cows to the cowshed and milking them, my mother brought for me a palmful of wild strawberries she had picked on the way. They were tiny but packed with flavor. While my older sisters could boast to the city kids that they milked cows, my less prestigious job was to pump water into a tank for them. First, I had to prime the pump by taking some water from the tank with a tin can. As I pumped, I watched the black water beetles skitter over the surface supported by water suspension. Then, "Aoogah, Aoogah! Dive, Dive!" they shot to the bottom. Water spiders flitted across the surface. Sometimes a luminescent lacy winged dragonfly came to visit.

In fall, a row of trees sported their bright colors behind me. In order to admire their beauty while I worked, I turned around and pumped with my hands behind my back. If I finished pumping before the cows had been milked, I could roam around the pasture to pick prickly gooseberries, red raspberries, blackberries, and hazelnuts, and to explore rocks and wildflowers. I brought along a wildflower book from the school library to identify them by name. I always hoped I would discover a new species and become famous for doing so. When I could see my mother coming from the cowshed, I raced back, inhaling the scent of the lavender bergamot that appeared to float in the evening mist.

At the end of summer, we herded the cows back to the farm. When I turned ten, I had to drive seven or eight cows home myself with a younger sibling who had not done it before, which I saw as an added responsibility. I was so afraid the cows would get away from me as we crossed the truss bridge over the Eau Claire River, the Chicago & Northwestern railroad tracks, and State Highway 29. It was also important to keep the cows out of the neighbors' yards and fields along the way. When we met a car on the road, I had to guide the cows to the side, but not let them stray. Then I remembered how easy it was to intimidate and control a dumb cow simply by tapping its side lightly with a dried mullein stalk. Nevertheless, I was relieved and felt a sense of accomplishment as the mile-and-a-half-long journey was completed.

We drank raw milk and could not bear the taste of pasteurized milk. When the cows ate acorns in late summer, it made the milk taste bitter. Our cows were tested regularly to ensure they bore no disease, not only for our own well being but also that of our market.

On the way to visit my Grandma and Grandpa Damask, we stopped in Shantytown for an ice cream cone at the small grocery store owned by our paternal Great Aunt Katy. How lovely was the curved scoop of pink ice cream brimming the cake cone. But alas! My mother's thumb mashed the round mound down into the base of the cone so it wouldn't drip on our clothes. She had spent a considerable amount of time and effort laundering, starching and ironing those dresses and wanted us to look presentable to Grandma. The practical overruled the aesthetic. Not to read too much into this, but perhaps it is a metaphor for why we survived. Certainly Maslow would agree.

When we arrived at Grandma's, her son said, "Here comes Susie and her calves." It was then that I realized how lucky we were to be allowed to drink as much milk as we wanted. At Grandma's, milk for the children was rationed to bring in more profit from the creamery.

We liked to visit Grandma and Grandpa Damask. Grandma was so happy to see us and always gave each of us a great big hug when we arrived, even though we were her step-grandchildren. She served us root beer floats as we sat in Adirondack chairs on the expansive lawn. It made us feel very special to be served by an adult. She had good taste in decorating and, besides her vegetable garden, had the most beautiful flower garden I had ever seen. There was always something in bloom, from the first crocus to the last chrysanthemum. Grandfather Leo had Belgian draft horses instead of a tractor. He said he liked their company out in the field and that they never broke down or required gasoline. They had a beautiful Collie named "Dewey" who nipped at the heels of the cows to bring them in for milking. A windmill pumped the water into the tank for the animals.

Although visiting and receiving relatives was our primary form of entertainment, my dad liked to watch airplanes take off and land at the Wausau Municipal Airport. On a Sunday afternoon, he would take the whole family out there. My mother would pack a lunch in a round tin from a fruitcake her sister had sent her for Christmas. Afterward, we would stop for an A&W Root Beer.

One summer a little private plane had engine trouble as it flew over our farm and made an emergency landing in the field behind our garage. "Get the camera!" my father shouted to my mother. Excitedly, my father helped the pilot partially disassemble the plane and offered to drive it in his trailer to Wausau. The grateful pilot offered to pay my dad, but he refused. It was the custom then to help people out without expecting anything in return. The pilot then promised my dad that after the plane was repaired, he would take every member of our family for a flight over our farm. The summer passed and my father doubted the pilot would keep his promise. But the following summer, true to his word, the pilot took us out three at a time on two separate trips. That was my very first plane flight. What a thrill it was to see our farm from this vantage point!

I'm on the far right with a carefully folded handkerchief in my pocket. It was a hot day with no place to sit.

After the dates on the catalogs expired, we cut out the figures in underwear and mounted them on cardboard from cereal boxes. Then we looked through the rest of the catalog to find and cut out apparel that matched the pose, and voila! We had free paper dolls. We placed them on a rectangular rag rug which served as a church in the morning and a swimming pool in the afternoon. When the paper dolls donned long evening gowns, the rug was transformed into a ballroom.

Grumpy, on the far right, because I got the smallest tub.

On hot days, my mother would place three tubs with water out on the grass near the house for the three of us oldest girls to cool off in. It was nice, but on a snapshot, I display a sour face. "Why do I always get the smallest tub?" I grumbled. "Because you are the smallest," my mother answered. This did not sit well with me because I couldn't help it I was the smallest.

In 1950, when I was nine, my parents bought the farm from my grandparents. The deed stipulated the sum (about $7,000) and several conditions. One was that my parents furnish all the milk, meat, and potatoes for my grandparents for the rest of their lives; another was that my grandparents could live rent-free in the part of the house where they were then living.

After the sale had been completed, we moved entirely into our own part of the house. My mother unpacked her wedding gifts (mostly enameled pots and pans) and we began to cook and eat our meals independently of our grandparents. The following summer, we got electricity, though we didn't have running water until after I left home. An electric motor now replaced the gas one in the wringer washing machine, and more importantly, my mother now had a refrigerator. This refrigerator lasted for at least thirty years since my

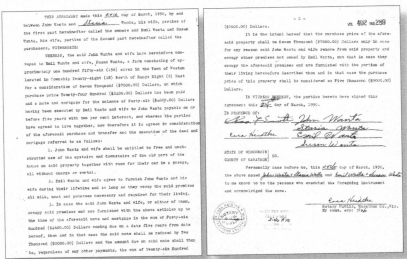

Two-page deed showing cost of farm and accompanying obligations.

father eventually replaced the burned out motor and the crumbling gasket around the door.

A cousin of my father's whose hobby was electronics provided us with a radio. *Sergeant Preston of the Yukon*, with his "Mush, you huskies," and *The Lone Ranger*, accompanied by the William Tell Overture, charged into our kitchen. *Dragnet*, with its "names have been changed to protect the innocent" also visited with its opening signature theme, the ominous "Dum - - - de - DUM - DUM." We did not have a television until a number of years later. This was partly because there was no local TV station, and partly because the cost was prohibitive.

We were lucky Grandpa let us use his Model A Ford until Dad was able to buy his own car in 1954. Dad pored over the brochures anticipating his first brand new car. He dropped the option of having a radio in it to bring the price down, even by a little bit. When he had saved enough, he tried to buy a maroon Ford Sedan, cash in hand. He was shocked, incredulous, and angry that the dealer would not accept cold hard cash. I'm not sure how they resolved it, because my parents never had a checking account. All I know is we got the car.

My mother always hung the clothes outside, even in winter. When the long underwear froze on the line and she brought it in, the ends of the long sleeves looked like frozen claws. If they were straightened out before they thawed, the threads would break, causing a tear in the fabric. After my parents sold the farm to a developer, the association that governed the homeowners stated that no clothes could be hung outdoors on clothes lines. Since my parents retained a lot, that really bothered my mother, but she recognized that by selling the land they had lost control of it.

They made the sale and built a new house in 1972. For the first time, my mother had new kitchen cupboards and counters. She also for the first time had an automatic washer and dryer. Ironically, she now had no children's clothes, diapers, or farm clothes to launder. The new house was a quarter mile north of the old farm, and the move took just a few trips, loading their belongings on the flatbed and hauling them to the new house.

As my mother sorted and packed her belongings, she held in her hands her old school workbooks and said to me, "I guess I'll throw these away." Of course, I wanted them. When I opened one, there were the various species of fall leaves, which together she and I had pressed when I had been a preschooler. Recently, I donated the workbooks to the Portage County Historical Society and the University of Wisconsin in Stevens Point.

Children of our economic class did not go to college, and neither my parents nor I had the faintest idea of where one might be located. Everything I was taught was geared to repeat my mother's life; we all assumed that society would not change much in the interim. I learned to knit, crochet, and embroider; to sew, iron, and clean house. Once I acquired these skills, I became bored. Why do something over and over again once you know how to do it?

We were trained to work, not talk about it. It was impossible to charm one's way into or out of anything. What one did was more important than what one said. It seemed the opposite when, as an adult, I worked for a major corporation. I had to adjust. In my job searches it was expected to tout one's accomplishments, whereas I had been schooled to be self-effacing. The work ethic I had acquired served me well most of my life, though at times I succumbed to hubris, resulting in personal injury. I also learned that being conscientious attracted a heavier workload and tighter deadlines. I saw this as a sign of high regard, and was proud to meet the challenge.

As a child, I thought my small world was the universe. By the time I was fourteen, I knew it was a small world and made a major life decision to enter the convent. My mother objected, but I insisted. It may seem hard to believe, but it was a bigger world for me, and to be sure, an adventure.

Epilogue

The convent which I entered in 1956 closed in July of 2019, and the building sold in 2021. I didn't realize it then, but that period of time in the convent was a microcosm of what was going on in religious orders across America. Religious orders were at their height when I entered and began to decline in the late1960s. Our order changed its garb in the 1960s, and the social apostolate began replacing the teaching ministry when I worked in Louisiana. I left the order in the late 1970s, almost ten years later than most members left. Religious life was a phenomenon which served a purpose at a time before the Peace Corps and NGO's were established. In *Called to Serve: A History of Nuns in America,* Margaret M. McGuiness writes: "The number of sisters in the United States had decreased from over 180,000 in 1966 to 128,000 in the 1990s with only one percent under the age of 30." This is good source which accurately describes the history of religious life in the United States as I lived it.

The graphics I had designed so painstakingly with T-square, triangle and exacto knives can now be executed by the click of computer keys. In fact, the Fortune 500 company I worked for has also dissolved.

My dad sold the cow pasture with all its memories, and it is now a housing development. The trillions of trilliums, once protected by state law, are no more. Since the sale of the farm in 1984, the farmhouse, barn and outlying buildings have all been razed. Highway 29 has been eclipsed by Highway 51 which runs as its parallel to the south. The Chicago and Northwestern railroad line was discontinued and the tracks torn out. The truss bridge over the Eau Claire River was demolished and relocated to another section of the river in the form of a small basic beam bridge that looks like any other you may have seen. The small mission church has been replaced by a contemporary place of worship and Upper Kelley school, which had been sold for a dollar, has since been replaced by a housing development. All the things and people who meant so much to me will be less than a speck in history.

My father died in 2001. The last thing I did for him was tie his shoes when his rheumatoid arthritis prevented him from doing so. My mother died in 2021 at the age of 103. Sadly, when she finally had time to read, she had become blind.

Besides my friendships, the most satisfying things in my life have been visiting Russia, working in the Deep South, spending time in New York, and of course, painting pictures. Had I known the foreign service existed, I probably would have joined it, and tried to after leaving the convent, but at the time the age limit was thirty-five, and I was thirty-six.

Now at age seventy-nine, after conquering cancer and hydrocephalus, I too, in due time will join these passages. Only my paintings will remain testimony to my existence. Since many of my art clients have died, happily my paintings continue to bring pleasure to their children. My art will be my legacy.

Acknowledgements

The first draft of this book was written in 1986 at the behest of a good friend who read chapters in their developmental stages. Life intervened, and I had to put the writing aside more than once. Of course, when I picked it up again, there were more experiences to record. So it is a never-ending process.

While I am grateful to my parents for life and how how hard they worked to provide for me, I am also grateful to Lorayne and Richard Radde who gave me a second life by supporting me in a myriad of ways. I also want to thank their daughter Rachel Schmidt-Radde, an editor in her own right, who graciously provided early editing.

Other readers who provided feedback for various chapters were Patricia Woodbury, Karen Kustritz, Dan Reed, Rosemary Willett, Peggy Stenborg, and Liz Williams.Vera Rooney provided written observations and encouragement. Dorothy Sherfinski verified facts and provided new information when I was in doubt about our school experiences. Mary Verity supplied the class photo of my much beloved one room school. My sister Evelyn refreshed my memory of some childhood circumstances. I am grateful to all of them. If there are any misrepresentations, they are solely my errors.

John Toren was a godsend as editor and designer of the entire book, offering suggestions and patiently addressing ever changing additions and subtractions.

Selected Bibliography

Baltimore Catechism No. 1, Official Revised Edition, Rev. Michael
   A. MacGuire, Benziger Brothers, Inc. New York, 1941.
Called to Serve: A History of Nuns in America, Margaret M.
   McGuiness, New York University Press. Washington Square,
   New York, NY, 2013.
Doubt, John Patrick Shanley, premiered at Manhattan Theatre
   Club, New York, NY, 2004.
Memoirs, David Rockefeller, Random House, New York, 2002.
Sisters, Catholic Nuns and the Making of America, John Fialka, St.
   Martins Press, 175 Fifth Avenue, New York, NY., 2003.
The Snowball: Warren Buffet and the Business of Life, Alice
   Schroeder, Bantam Books, 2008.

Made in USA - Kendallville, IN
28453_9798772032527
12.13.2021 1335